Wm. A. Cleeveland

Helping Children with the Mystery of Death

Elizabeth Liggett Reed

 ABINGDON
Nashville

HELPING CHILDREN WITH THE MYSTERY OF DEATH

ISBN 0-687-16837-6

Library of Congress Catalog Card Number: 79-98897

MANUFACTURED BY THE PARTHENON PRESS AT
NASHVILLE, TENNESSEE, UNITED STATES OF AMERICA

TO JULIET
   my sister who helped me
   with the mystery of death
   this book is gratefully dedicated

FOREWORD

Death, the great universal experience, is a subject which many people push into the background as though if it were ignored it might go away, at least for a long time.

Some parents try to protect their children against the reality of death by not talking about it and, as much as possible, by keeping them from direct experience with death when it touches their lives. As a result, when death suddenly becomes unavoidable in a child's experience he is totally unprepared to meet it, and, therefore, it frequently has traumatic effects, often extending into his adult years.

Today children cannot be shielded from the fact of death, even if we wished to do so. Through mass media it confronts them almost daily. Television brings it into our living rooms, often in its most violent forms. Children's questions and comments show that it is a subject of deep concern to them.

How can parents and teachers answer their children's questions about this great mystery? And how can they help them when death comes into their experience? All the great religions and many great souls can help us with the *what* to say to children about death and about life, for death is a part of life; neither one can be considered apart from the other. And through the findings of child study and psychology we can learn a great deal about *how* to help children when they face and must live through an experience of death—how to help them in such a way that through the experience, however painful, they may grow in understanding and in strength.

The purpose of this book is to help with the *what to tell* children about death, to suggest experiences which will help prepare them to meet death, and to give guidance for the time when a child must suffer through an experience of death. The illustrations in it are all true stories. It is written especially for those who hold the Christian belief about life and life after death, but it contains material which has been helpful to those of other faiths and to those with no religious belief.

ACKNOWLEDGMENTS

I am deeply indebted to many friends for invaluable help in the writing of this book. Among them are ministers, directors and teachers of Christian education, public school educators, editors, and parents —fathers and mothers with various backgrounds and interests. They read the manuscript, gave their criticisms and suggestions, and contributed illustrations from their personal experiences. They are an integral part of this book. Though they are too many to name individually, I wish to express to each of them my great appreciation and gratitude.

CONTENTS

Helping Children with the Mystery of Death

Resource Materials for Use with Children

Enriching Materials for Adults

HELPING CHILDREN
WITH THE MYSTERY
OF DEATH

1
FACING DEATH WITH CHILDREN

A recent study of children's fears[1] revealed the fact that 80 percent of their fears were concerned with death; the children worried about dying or being killed or about someone in their family dying. In another study of children's questions in the field of religion,[2] the children asked more questions about death than about any other subject.

Parents are well aware at what an early age in a child's life these questions begin. "Why do people die?" wondered a four-year-old boy, and a five-year-old asked, "Does everybody die, Mommie? Will you die? Will Daddy die? When?"

When a child inquires about death, we need first to ask ourselves why he is asking. Frequently his immediate need is not an intellectual explanation in answer to his question but an unexpressed need for reassurance and emotional security. Back of a child's questions about death often lies anxiety or fear—fear

[1] Study by Dr. Eve Allina Lazar for the National Institute of Mental Health, quoted in *New York Times Magazine*, September 22, 1968, p. 109.

[2] Committee on Children's Work, Commission on General Christian Education, National Council of the Churches, 1962.

13

that those he loves and who care for him may die and he will be left alone. Our first response may need to be one of understanding and reassurance. Perhaps we could bring his anxiety into the open by saying, "Why do you ask?" If the child is older and there is not time to discuss his question adequately, you might tell him, "You have asked a very important question. It is a question about which people have always wondered. We will talk more about it this evening." If this is suggested it is very important that it be done then, or the child is likely to conclude that the subject is being avoided because it is something to be feared. It could be a significant experience if both parents would participate in an unhurried discussion of this great mystery, sharing freely their thoughts and faith and saying frankly "I don't know" to some questions their child might ask.

Children personalize what they hear. If they hear that the parent of some child has died, they, with their lively imaginations, immediately picture it as happening to their parents.

Usually children's fears are not expressed; children worry in silence, sometimes over long periods of time. Often those closest to a child do not suspect the anxiety with which he is living, nor do they have any idea that something is troubling him. One father of a sensitive ten-year-old boy sometimes at bedtime would say, "Is there anything that is troubling you tonight?" We who would help children need to be sensitive to their moods as well as to listen to what they are saying.

Children are aware of their dependency, and in their ignorance and inexperience they fear the unknown. The reason for a child's fear may not be real, but the fear is real. When we encourage a child to express his anxiety and accept his fears and his feelings, he has a sense of safety in our understanding. Frances Wicks, in *The Inner World of Childhood,* says, "The child in a measure substitutes the security of the sympathetic relationship for the unknown fear."

A small boy worried himself sick for fear that his parents had been killed when they were delayed in returning from a short trip. When they came they found him wrapped in a blanket, huddled by the fire. When he was a little older he still worried for fear they would die, and he tried to work out a plan for just what he would do if they should die. He decided that he could walk some twenty-five miles to a children's home which he had seen. Fortunately his mother discovered his anxiety and assured him that it was not likely they would die, but if ever they should, an aunt who loved him would come and take care of him. His mother told him that their next-door neighbor had his aunt's telephone number and would keep him until she came for him.

Some parents show their wills to their children and let them read the provision which has been made for them in case their parents should die. In one family the children had an opinion in choosing the person with whom they would live if both their parents died.

Children need to know that in addition to their parents they are loved by many people—relatives and friends. Here the fellowship of the church and synagogue can play an important role in giving the child a sense of security; they can fulfill an essential function in meeting the need in a one-parent family.

The father of five-year-old Bob and two-year-old Larry died in an accident. The Sunday after his funeral when the boys arrived at their church school classrooms, each was greeted not only by his teacher, who was a woman, but also by a man. Larry soon climbed into the lap of his new friend and remained there throughout the session. In the weeks that followed, Larry and Bob found that they could count on these friends being there each Sunday; and during the seven years since that day the church has seen to it that there was a man teacher, a father figure, in each of their classes. Always children's foremost need is for love and assurance of continuing love and care.

Knowledge helps give security; lack of simple facts is the source of many childhood fears. Ignorance of facts in a crisis or a disturbing situation increases a child's feeling of helplessness, and asking questions may be his way of seeking reassurance. Simple information given truthfully without evasion or embarrassment often releases a child from some imaginary anxiety. A five-year-old boy was told when his grandfather died that he had become very tired and had "gone to sleep." The child, of course, sensed that there was something quite different about this kind of sleep since he no longer saw his grandfather. For weeks his bedtime became an unhappy experience, until his parents discovered that he was fighting sleep because he feared that he would fall into the same kind of sleep his grandfather had and would not wake up again.

Even a small child, when a person whom he loves dies, needs to be told the truth: that the person has died, that he still loves him, but that he cannot come back to him. He accepts this fact much better than being left with the feeling that the person he loved did not care enough and has deserted him or "gone away" without telling him "good-bye."

Elizabeth was four years old when her father died. No one told her that he had died; he just disappeared. Three years later, when she was seven, she began having tantrums whenever her mother went away without her. She was consistently punished, but the tantrums continued. No one suspected that they were caused by the fear that her mother also would disappear and she would never see her again.

Children may not be able to comprehend all that we say, and very young children do not accept the finality of death, but they will find assurance in our forthright attitude and in our honesty in answering their questions. And they will then feel free to turn to us later when other questions arise in their minds. A father who had tried to answer the questions of his little girl about God remarked afterward, "I may not have helped her to understand God better, but at least she had the experience of talking with someone who was honest with her."

If we make ourselves available to children, listen, encourage questions, are sensitive to their feelings, and take time to "talk it out," always leaving the door open for further conversation on the subject, then children's fears and anxieties will not be pushed back to become buried in their subconscious and cause disturbance in later years.

Parents and teachers who have the security which is rooted in a dynamic faith and believe in a life after death communicate this confidence to their children. We saw this demonstrated so inspiringly when Martin Luther King, Jr., was killed. Mrs. King, with her great faith and courage, told how their children had said, "Daddy is not dead. His body is dead but his spirit can never die."

In helping children with the problem of death, we need to have some understanding of what death means to children of different ages. Sylvia Anthony was the first investigator to work directly with children in a study of their understanding of death. In 1940 she made a study with 123 children between the ages of three and twelve years. She found that death thoughts are frequent in children of school age; they appear in children's fantasies, in their play, and in their response to suggestions of fear and separation. She

learned that children between five and six years begin to have some idea of the meaning of death; by
seven years their concept is much more advanced; between eight and nine years they have some logical
and biological understanding; and at twelve they are
beginning to develop a more mature concept.

In 1948 Marie Nagy in Hungary made a study of
children's concepts, working with 378 children between the ages of three and ten years. Her investiga-
tion showed that children tend to pass through three
developmental stages in their understanding of death:

Stage One. Young children under five do not accept
death as final. It is like sleep: you die, then you wake
up again; or like going on a journey: you go away,
then you come back. This was illustrated when three-
year-old John Kennedy, some time after his father's
funeral, met his father's secretary and asked, "When
is my Daddy coming back?" One four-year-old expressed it, "You get sick and die and go to heaven,
but you can come back for visits."

Stage Two. Children from five to nine gradually
learn to accept the finality of death for someone who
has died, but they are slow to think of it as something
which happens to everyone and which will happen
to them. The idea that they will die generally comes
slowly to children. Miss Nagy found that one third
of the children in this age bracket personified death:
they conceived of death as a person, the "death-man,"
or a ghost figure. They associated him with darkness
and night. Death was not inevitable; only those die

whom the "death-man" catches and carries off. Whoever can get away does so.

Stage Three. Around nine or ten, children recognize the fact that death is universal and inevitable,
and that sometime they too will die. A boy this age
wrote: "What is death? Well, I think it is a part of a
person's life. Like school. Life has many parts. Only
one part of it is earthly. As in school, we go on to a
different class. To die means to begin a new life.
Everyone has to die once, but the soul lives on."

Two conclusions seem to be indicated from various
studies of children's understandings and attitudes
about death:

1. The children most concerned about the problem of death are the younger children up to
   seven years of age. The more secure a person is
   in himself and in his role in life, the less he
   seems concerned about death. Perhaps one
   reason for the child's greater concern at this age
   is the fact that he is leaving the security of his
   home and is in the process of finding himself in
   the larger world of school and playground. Between nine and eleven, "the golden age," when
   children's roles are generally well-defined, the
   concern about death recedes and does not re-
   appear until adolescence, when again they are
   going through a period of change and adjust-
   ment.

2. Children fear death less for themselves than they fear that their parents or those they love and those who care for them may die and leave them alone. A typical question was asked by a five-year-old boy: "Mother, what would happen to us if you and Daddy were killed?"

Very often a child's first experience in facing death occurs when a pet dies. Children have deep affection for their pets, and when they die, children not only grieve over their loss, but they are concerned about what has happened to them. "Do dogs go to heaven?" asked a troubled four-year-old. And the nine-year-old son of a farmer wanted to know, "What happens to animals when they die? Do they go to heaven where people are?"

Since children love their pets they feel sure God also must love them. They understand Jesus' words, "And not one of them is forgotten before God" (Luke 12:6). Seven-year-old Kathy, when her pet goldfish died, buried it and then made a sign for the grave on which she wrote: "He is rose. God loves him."

Margueritte Bro tells about five-year-old Edwin when his dog Bridget was killed. One weekend when his mother and father were away and Great-aunt Hester was taking care of him, Bridget was run over by a truck. After Edwin had spent his first grief and Aunt Hester had telephoned his father what had happened, Edwin's questions began: "Where did Bridget's soul go, Auntie? Has she gone to heaven?"

Aunt Hester was not able to comfort him; she ruled out any possibility that Bridget might be in heaven because "the Bible doesn't say anything about animals in heaven."

It was nearly midnight when Father drove in. Edwin, sleeping fitfully, heard the car on the driveway. He might have known his father would come back. He scrambled out of bed and by that time his father was coming through the bedroom door followed by Aunt Hester. Edwin jumped into his father's arms and neither of them said anything. They just hugged each other. Finally Edwin slid down from his father's arms. "It's tough, isn't it?" he said. "It's tough that nobody could bark when you drove in."

"You bet it's tough, son."

"Father, she didn't go to heaven." Edwin reached desperately for his father's hand when he heard himself saying the words. "She's dead but God didn't want her."

"Who says she didn't go to heaven?" asked Father sternly.

"Auntie says that heaven is no place for animals. It doesn't say a thing about them in the Bible."

"Oh, that—" Father dismissed the matter with a gesture. "It doesn't have to say anything about them in the Bible because it says that God is our Father and we expect a father to look after his children's dogs and other pets." . . . [To Aunt Hester's protest he said,] "You'd look after a puppy in need any time one came your way, my dear. I'm just allowing God to be as friendly as we humans are."

Then Father turned to Edwin, speaking seriously. "I don't understand a lot about heaven, Son, except that I believe that whatever happens after we're dead is all right. Do you know what I mean? It may be all different from anything we know now. But whatever it is, God will do the right thing by all of us. Men, women, boys, girls, babies, dogs,—everybody. After all, if God is love, we don't have to be anxious about his taking care of us. That's the way I see it. . . . Tomorrow we'll talk about it some more. We're sure going to miss little Bridget, but wherever she is, it's okay with her."

"Okay," said Edwin, drawing a long breath which was both a spent sob and a yawn. He could go to sleep now, really to sleep, and figure out the rest in the morning. Tomorrow he'd miss Bridget just as much, but he could stand missing her if everything was okay with Bridget.[3]

Parents will help their children in facing death if they can talk naturally with them about it before an emotional crisis arises. Children have insatiable curiosity. Many casual occasions occur, such as driving past a cemetery or looking at a newspaper picture of someone who has died, when parents and children have an opportunity to talk unemotionally about death; children can ask the questions which puzzle them and parents can share their thoughts and faith.

[3] From pp. 108-11 in *When Children Ask,* rev. ed., by Margueritte Harmon Bro. Copyright 1940, 1956 by Margueritte Harmon Bro. Reprinted by permission of Harper & Row, Publishers.

Then children may begin to realize that death is a part of life—one of life's great mysteries, a mystery which some people think of as life's supreme adventure, a mystery which we feel we can trust to the God who gave us life.

2

INTERPRETING DEATH TO CHILDREN

How we interpret death to children will depend upon what we ourselves think and feel about death; our children will sense what we really think and how we feel. They live in a world of feeling, and they are uncanny in their intuitive understanding of our true feelings.

Our attitude toward death is inseparably bound up with our attitude toward life; they are two sides of the same coin. If for us life is an opportunity to grow, to give, and to receive in all of life's relationships, if we are seekers after truth and are faithful in living out the truth as we see it, we shall probably think of ourselves as spiritual persons now living in a physical body, a habitation which we know one day will perish.

John Quincy Adams at the age of eighty met an old friend on a street in Boston. "How are you today, John Quincy Adams?" asked his friend. With a twinkle in his eyes, the ex-president replied: "John Quincy Adams is very well, thank you. But the house in which he lives is becoming dilapidated; it is tottering on its foundation. I think John Quincy Adams will have to move out of it before very long. But he, himself, is very well, thank you."

Edwin Markham, America's poet laureate, in a funeral address said, "The few short years we spend on earth are only the first scene in a divine drama that extends on into eternity." When this is our conviction, the children sense it, and we do not shy away from talking with them about death.

If a parent does not believe in a future life, he can help his child best by being humbly honest with him and, at the same time, see to it that he has the opportunity to learn about the faith of those who do believe. Thus, the door will be open for him to search and find his own faith.

A mother who had been brought up as an atheist felt that she would never change. But realizing that she had an obligation to see that her son had an honest exposure to a religious faith, she sent him to a liberal church school. The result was that, in the course of years, both she and her son became active members of this church.

A young child who is without any experience of death finds it puzzling to understand what death is. Wendy, a four-year-old, said to her grandmother, "Nanny, what is death?" "Wendy, it is when *you* leave your body," replied her grandmother. "Oh, thank you, Nanny, no one had explained it to me before." This was sufficient for Wendy, but for some children it may be necessary to explain further that death means that the body doesn't work any more— the legs don't run, the eyes can't see, the ears can't hear, the heart stops beating; the part of the person that says "I" has left the body because it could not work any more.

Four-year-old Ann's grandfather had been both father and grandfather to her for as long as she could remember. They were living at the seashore the summer he died. The morning Ann was told that during the night Grandfather had died, that his body had become so sick that Grandfather had had to leave it, Ann's first reaction was one of anger. Her mother told her that he must be very happy in the new world to which he had gone for there were many there who loved him and he would not suffer any more. His body was left behind just as the beautiful seashells, out of which life had gone, were left on the beach. As Ann thought about these new ideas her anger seemed to leave her. She wanted to see Grandfather's "shell." Carrying Ann in her arms her mother took her into Grandfather's room. Ann did not speak as she looked down at the still form on the bed; then with tears rolling down her cheeks she smiled. A little later she asked again to see Grandfather's body. After her second visit Ann accepted the fact of his death, and there was no more anger.

"Why do people die?" asks the young child, especially the four- and five-year-olds. Children of kindergarten age are trusting, and they accept the fact that death is a part of the plan for all life; life includes birth, growth, change, and an end to life as we know it here. If people did not die when they became very old, there would not be enough room in the world for new babies to come and grow up. God has planned for the birth of babies, for their growth, and has provided richly for all our needs in this world. We can trust him that his plan for death is good also. The Bible says that "whether we live or whether we die, we are the Lord's" (Rom. 14:8).

Michael was four when his grandmother was dying. They had been very close, and his parents were worried about how her death would affect him. His mother wrote:

Thus it was with considerable trepidation that we approached Grandmother's house that Sunday after Easter. We arrived to find her sleeping. My husband and Michael went into the bedroom. Grandma opened her eyes for a moment at the sound of their voices, stretched out her hand to Michael and closed her eyes again.

A half hour later we all realized that Grandma was dead.

As I was preparing to take the children home . . . Grandpa approached Michael.

"Come, Michael," he said, leading him toward the bedroom, "We'll say good-bye to Grandma."

My husband and I exchanged a worried glance, but said nothing.

There in the large sunny bedroom . . . these two—old man and little boy—said "good-bye."

"Grandma died," Michael said later. "It was her time to." And so our oldest child learned about death in a quiet and familiar room. And my husband and I will always be grateful to Grandpa for making this gentle acceptance of death possible for our son.[1]

Children are aware that not all who die are old. Sometimes a playmate or the parent of some child dies. It is best to give them the simple, physical reason for the death. We can tell children that we do not yet know how to cure some diseases; doctors and scientists are working, trying to find the cause and cure. We might add that no doubt there are children today who will become doctors when they grow up, and they will study and make discoveries that will prevent or cure diseases.

It is most important to avoid such explanations as "God took him." Helen and Lewis Sherrill write:

There is a body of popular ideas about the cause of death which often do great damage if used with children. . . . These ideas commonly attribute the cause of death to God, and in presenting the matter in this light we run the risk of picturing God as an enemy who may strike us down. Under such teaching a child sometimes develops an intense hatred of God which he then fears to express, with the result that he has an unnecessary burden of guilt to carry in addition to the sorrow. Instead we should draw upon the concepts which we have already tried to give the child: i.e., that God is always

[1] Ann A. Buzynski, "It Was Her Time," in *Baby Talk*, Jan., 1969, p. 34.

with people in life and continues to be with them in death . . . as a loving Father.[2]

In one study of children's questions about death, the question asked most frequently by children from three to twelve years old was, "What happens to people after they die?" And over and over again came questions about heaven: "Where is heaven?" "What is heaven like?" "How do you get there?"

We can tell them, "Heaven is where God is. 'God is love' and the life of heaven is a life of love. This life, the life of heaven, should begin here and now. Wherever and whenever we choose the way of love and walk in it, we begin to live the kind of life which is heaven. The Bible calls it 'eternal life,' the life which lasts forever because it is life in God who is love." If we use the expression "life forever" we will help the children to think of heaven not so much as a place, but as life lived in love, life here and life beyond our earth life. Children will understand this; they know that nothing is more important than love.

We can help children to realize that this world is a wonderful place in which to grow in love. We can encourage them to think of the opportunities they have each day to practice love in their home, at school, and on the playground. Besides thinking of the kind and helpful things they can do for others, help them to

[2] "Interpreting Death to Children," a pamphlet published for the Division of Christian Education by the Department of Publication Services of the National Council of the Churches of Christ.

think of the chance they sometimes have of doing something much harder—perhaps forgiving someone who has been unkind to them. Whenever we love unselfishly, we help to make this world more like heaven. And then when it comes time for us to leave our physical body, the house we now live in, we will feel at home and happy in heaven; and in the life forever we will continue to grow in love.

When children press us, as they often do, for concrete details about life in heaven, we can tell them that we do not know. If all our questions about life in the next world could be answered, we would not understand any more than the baby in its mother's womb could imagine and understand the world into which it is to be born. We have to wait until we go to the next world to discover all the wonders God has planned for us. The Bible says: "Things beyond our seeing, things beyond our hearing, things beyond our imagining, all prepared by God for those who love him" (I Cor. 2:9b NEB).

One Sunday morning, a fourth grade class of boys and girls listened to their minister preach a sermon on death. The following Sunday when they came together in their church school class, their teacher with no preliminary discussion asked two questions, "What is heaven?" and "What is hell?" Quickly came the following responses:

"Heaven is where people go if they care about others."

"Hell is where a person cares only about himself."

"Heaven is a place where people aren't mean to each other."

"Hell is where everyone is against you."

"Heaven is not a place. It's love."

"Hell is hate."

Many children's questions reveal a great deal of confusion about what happens to the body when a person dies and what happens to the person himself. A six-year-old boy asked, "If Grandpa went to heaven, why did we put him in the ground?" And an eight-year-old said: "What I want to know is how a person gets out of that casket? Do they go out before it's closed up or do they wait for God to come and let them out?" On the other hand, when parents talk with their children and help them to distinguish between the "I" that thinks and loves and the body in which the "I" lives, they seem quick to understand.

Long ago a mother wrote about her little boy who, after his grandfather died, was sobbing in bed one night. "I'm afraid Grandfather is cold down there in the ground," he said. His mother replied, "See your clothes on the chair—do you think they are cold? They are like Grandfather's body. Grandfather lived in his body, then his body wore out as your clothes wear out; it could not be mended any more. But the part of Grandfather that we love is living with God." The six-year-old son of a college chaplain during a conversation about cemeteries remarked, "Why does anybody want to know where your dead body is buried?"

Seven-year-old Ruth came to her mother one day and said, "Where is the really me?" When she was nine, she put her thoughts into the following poem:

> Where is the really, really me?
> I'm somewhere, I know, but where can that be?
> I'm not my nose, nor my mouth, nor my eye,
> I'm not my feet, nor my leg, nor my thigh.
> I'm not my hand, nor my arm, nor my hip,
> And I'm not my teeth, nor my tongue, nor my lip.
> I'm sure I'm not my elbow or knee—
> Oh, where am I? Oh, where can I be? [3]

Nancy was five when her father, who had seemed so well when he kissed her goodnight, died of a sudden heart attack after she had gone to bed. Nancy did not see that her father's room was empty when early the next morning a friend of the family came to take her on a visit to her home in the country. Because her mother unfortunately had had no opportunity to prepare Nancy, she did not attend her father's funeral service. Late that afternoon when Nancy came home, her mother took her on her lap and said she had a poem written by a little girl that she wanted to read her. She read Ruth's poem, "Where Is the Really, Really Me?" Then they played

[3] By Ruth Fahs. Used by permission of her mother Sophia Lyon Fahs.

a game about it. Her mother, touching Nancy's nose, mouth, and eyes, etc., asked, "Is this Nancy's really, really me?" Nancy laughed and said that it was not. "Where," asked her mother, "is the part of Nancy that loves and thinks up happy things to do for people?" Nancy decided that her "really me" lived inside her "house" that people saw and could touch. Later when her fifteen-year-old brother came home for supper, Nancy ran to meet him and announced, "I have a new game I want to play with you."

It was the following morning that her mother again took Nancy on her knee and with her arm around her told her that Daddy's body, the "house" he had lived in, had become so ill in the night that he had had to leave it for a new "house." After answering Nancy's questions as simply as possible and saying to some, "I don't know but Daddy knows," her mother continued, "We will miss Daddy very much. And now the three of us will need to do for each other some of the things Daddy always did for us."

"Mother," said Nancy, "when I sneeze you must say, 'God bless you.' Daddy always did."

"Telling Nancy was so much easier than I thought it would be," said her mother afterward. "She seemed to understand."

Ruth's poem also helped a church school teacher when she talked with her class of first graders about Bobby, a member of the class who had died during the week. Sitting on one of the low chairs in a circle with the children she read, "Where Is the Really,

Really Me?" The children listened with some merriment, then they talked about "where is the really me?" —the part of us that thinks, loves, and chooses. Their body, they decided, was the "house" the really me lived in.

"Sometimes our house gets sick," said the teacher. Immediately everyone wanted to tell about the time when his "house" had been sick. After all had had an opportunity to talk, the teacher continued, "Sometimes the house gets so sick that it can't get well, then the really me has to leave his house and have a new house. That is what happened to Bobby this week." There was sorrowful silence in the group. Only Mary, who lived next door to Bobby and had been told of his death, showed strained distress.

The teacher explained briefly about the kind of sickness Bobby had had and said that doctors had not yet discovered how to cure it. "Perhaps some of you may become doctors when you grow up, and discover how to cure some sickness doctors do not yet know how to help." The children talked about what they would like to do when they grew up, and that day many wanted to be doctors and nurses.

In a closing service of worship the story "New Clothes for Old" (see "Resources for Use with Children") was told. That afternoon Mary's mother phoned the teacher to thank her for the help which had been given to Mary. "Mary," she said, "had been so upset that she had refused to accept the fact of her playmate's death." But she had come home from church school, said her mother, with peace in her heart.

In February a teacher learned that within a few months she would have to tell the children in her church school that their minister had died. In the six- to eight-year-old group, they began thinking together about the things we can always depend upon; day following night, spring following winter, harvest following seedtime.

They had conversations about change and growth in nature; a favorite story was "The Dragonfly Grubs" (see "Resources for Use with Children") . They talked about change and growth in themselves. "Where are the babies you used to be?" asked their teacher. "All gone," they said with a twinkle in their eyes. "But you are still here," said the teacher. "And someday where will be the boys and girls you are now?" "Oh, we will be grown up," came the quick reply. Change, they decided, is something we can always count upon because it is one of God's laws, part of his plan for our world. And in the group there was a happy attitude of confidence and anticipation toward changes to come.

It was a Sunday in May that the teacher told the children their minister had died that morning. She said that his body, the "house" he had lived in, had become so sick that it could not get well, so he had to leave it. "What his new body in the new life is like we do not know," she continued. "That is a surprise

God has for us. He knows now what that surprise is; and sometime we, too, shall know."

At the close of school that morning, seven-year-old Julie broke the news of his death to her mother and added, "We've been talking about change in our church school and, Mother, death is just another change."

Peter Marshall in a sermon on death told the story of a little boy who was ill with an incurable disease. His mother did all she could to keep him happy and unaware of the seriousness of his illness, but with a child's intuitive understanding, he gradually came to realize that he was going to die. One day he surprised his mother by asking, "Mother, what is it like to die? Mother, does it hurt?" His mother made a hasty flight into the kitchen, where she offered a hurried prayer for guidance and strength to help her child. Immediately she knew how she would answer his question.

"Kenneth," she said as she returned to the next room, "you remember when you were a tiny boy how you used to play so hard all day that when night came you would be too tired even to undress, and you would tumble into mother's bed and fall asleep? That was not your bed . . . it was not where you belonged. And you would only stay there for a little while. In the morning, much to your surprise, you would wake up and find yourself in your own room. You were there because someone had loved you and taken care of you. Your father had come—with big strong arms—and carried you away. Kenneth, death is just like that. We just wake up some morning to find ourselves in the other room—our own room where we belong—because the Lord Jesus loved us." The lad's shining, trusting face looking up into hers told her that the point had gone home and that there would be no more fear . . . only love and trust. . . . He never questioned again. And several weeks later he fell asleep just as she had said. "That," said Peter Marshall, "is what death is like." [4]

In our own experiences of helping children with the mystery of death we discover that often they are closer to the heart of reality than are adults. They seem to have an intuitive comprehension of truth, and their ability to trust life, accept and adjust to it, surprises us. Through the grace of their acceptance and trust, and in their wholehearted giving of themselves to the present, they become our teachers, and we understand the words of Jesus: "Unless you turn and become like children, you will never enter the kingdom of heaven" (Matt. 18:3).

[4] Catherine Marshall, *A Man Called Peter* (New York: McGraw-Hill Book Company, 1951), p. 273.

3
SHARING GRIEF WITH CHILDREN

Death always comes as a shock and brings a time of sorrow, even when it has been expected and is a welcome release from suffering for our loved one. There is profound grief when the young die before their life here has seemingly been fulfilled or when children are left without a parent. But in our deepest grief there can be the comfort of our faith that all is well with those who have gone. And though they are beyond the reach of our dull senses, we have confidence that they are not out of reach of our heart. Intuitively, we know that "love can never lose its own."

When death comes, children need to be allowed to share in our grief as well as in our faith. They can stand sorrow better than the isolation of being shut out through the mistaken idea that they should be spared suffering. During the Second World War in England, parents found that their children could take the danger and tragedies of the bombing better than they could stand separation from their parents when they were sent for safety to the country.

Grief demands expression. It is a mistaken idea to think that weeping is a sign of immaturity or lack of manliness. There is no need for embarrassment at an honest expression of emotion that is born of love; "the price of love is suffering." Jesus wept with the sorrowing Mary and her friends on their way to the tomb of Lazarus.

While we will want to protect children from inordinate grief, deep feeling frankly expressed and shared can be a strengthening bond between children and adults. Ten-year-old Mary told her teacher, "I loved my grandfather as much as I love my father. When he died no one told me. I saw my mother crying but I did not know why. When I found out that he had died, I locked myself in a room and would not let anyone in. I was crying, not because my grandfather had died, but because no one had told me."

When a loved person dies, a child has a right to know it, and he must be told within a reasonable time or relationships with those whom the child trusts may be damaged irreparably.

Grief demands not only expression but also time. It takes time to suffer grief and come through the experience a stronger, more understanding person. During a period of mourning people generally pass through three stages in their "grief work." There is first a short time of shock, usually lasting from the actual death through the burial of the body. This is followed by a period of acute grief, with restless sleep, loss of appetite and weight, sometimes accompanied by disorganization, withdrawal, and loss of interest in the ordinary affairs of life. Then comes a final period of reestablishment, and interests again turned outward.

For a healthy readjustment to life it is necessary that an experience of grief be lived through. If we refuse to accept and live with our grief or if, in our endeavor to be brave, we try to stifle and hurry through grief, we will pay for it later. "You tried to be too brave," a doctor told a young woman who, many months after the death of a loved one, was surprised to find herself on the verge of a breakdown.

Relatives and friends can perform an essential function. There is a mysterious lightening of the burden of sorrow when those who mourn are surrounded by people who love them and with whom they can talk. Children sense the warm love and support, and it gives them the security of knowing that there are many who love and care for them and their family. If the family is receiving friends at home, children can be given some definite responsibility such as opening the door, showing guests where to put their wraps, helping to serve simple refreshments. Something that needs to be done is a healing blessing for both children and adults.

Children, too, need to face and live through a grief. They need to have the opportunity and the freedom to ask questions which are on their minds and to "talk it out." Eight-year-old Jean's mother was killed in an auto accident. When well-meaning relatives tried not to talk about it in her presence, Jean burst out, "No one will talk with me. I want to talk about it."

Sometimes children, if they have been told that the person who has died has gone to heaven, cannot understand why people are crying. A ten-year-old boy seeing his grandmother weeping beside the casket of his grandfather asked, "Hasn't anyone told her Grandpa is with God and he is happy?" Children need to have it made clear that sorrow and tears are not for the person who has died but because he will be missed so much. One mother explained to her small son before they went to his grandfather's funeral that though he might see people crying, they would not be unhappy for Grandfather but only because they would miss seeing and talking with him.

There is much that children can learn from the way in which their family accepts and adjusts to a period of strain and grief. A mother of two elementary-age children whose aunt had lived with the family during a long and difficult last illness remarked, "It has been good for the children; it has been good for them to see how their father and I have managed."

Children have many different reactions to grief. Sometimes death is too great a shock for the young child to accept, and he denies it. In the story of Bobby referred to earlier in "Interpreting Death to Children," when the children in his school were told that he had died, Mary burst out, "It is not true! He is not dead." An unthinking adult reprimanded her for telling a falsehood. Understanding and gentleness are essential in times of shock and grief.

Because a young child is not able to grasp the significance of death he may appear callous to a person who does not understand; he is sorrowful for a little while, then he goes about his play apparently as though nothing had happened.

Older children nearly always suffer from some form of guilt when a person whom they love has died. They feel guilty because of a time when they were mad at the person, or because they did not do something the person asked them to. Not infrequently a child blames himself for the person's death. A boy who had repeatedly been asked to play quietly during his grandfather's last illness thought that he was responsible for his death because he had made so much noise. Young children believe in magic; they think that by wishing something they can make it happen. If at some time a child has said, "I wish you were dead," and later the person dies, he is likely to blame himself thinking his wish was the cause of death.

We need to help a child get rid of his guilt feelings. We can make an opportunity by opening the conversation and talking realistically about the person who has died, recalling not only the happy times they had together, but also a time when the child was mad at him. Let the child know that most people get angry at times with those they love. If you think the child blames himself for the death you might say, "Your angry feelings had nothing to do with his death. He understood; he knew that you loved him."

Some children take on physical manifestations of illness; they feel a tightness in the throat, they have a pain, they don't want to eat, they are restless sleepers.

Sometimes a child expresses the strain of grief through his physical behavior. He may become unusually noisy and boisterous and act in ways which seem inappropriate and unfeeling.

Anger and resentment are not unusual reactions. He may feel angry with the person who has died for leaving him, with the doctor for not making the patient well, or resentment toward God for letting him die. In his frustration and helplessness the child may show hostility toward those around him or strike out at some inanimate object; for example, he may kick a chair, smash a glass, or destroy a favorite toy.

During a period of grief and strain we need to provide children with opportunities for the release of strain through physical activities, out-of-doors if possible. When children have to be confined to the house, we can see that they have materials through which they can express their feelings creatively—clay, paints, finger paints, and large sheets of paper; making their pictures will be an outlet for their feelings. To the discerning adult their pictures will also reveal a great deal about the present state of those inner feelings.

During the days of mourning the routine of life needs to be kept as normal as possible. And there should be no feeling of guilt in providing for outings and play for the children. It is of utmost importance that the child be with someone who loves him and understands his needs. If he must go away from home for a short period, the reason for this should be explained to him and, if possible, he should be given some choice in the matter of with whom he will stay.

Should the young child attend the funeral or memorial service is a question which is frequently asked by parents. Generally, yes. Sometimes when death occurs in a family the young child is sent away to stay with family friends and does not return until after the funeral. There is danger in this; the child generally senses that something unusual has happened, and he feels excluded. Of course, how the situation is handled will depend upon the individual child and the circumstances, and young children should always be protected from a hysterical display of emotion. But with intelligent preparation, so that the child knows what is going to happen and what is expected of him, there can be lasting value for him in attending the service. He feels that he is part of an occasion which has great meaning for his family. He may not understand all that is happening, but he knows that he belongs and that together with "our" friends "we" are showing "our" love for the person who has died. The feeling of belonging, psychologists tell us, is most important to the emotional security of a child.

Those who saw the funeral service of Senator Robert Kennedy on television were aware of the significance of the service to the Kennedy children. One felt the strength in the solidarity of the family, and the recognition of the children as a vital part of it was evident when they took the bread to the altar for the Communion service. In the scripture and the music there was the triumphant assurance of the victory of life over death. In the Christian ritual of burial a note of joy is appropriate. Great hymns, such as "For All the Saints" (music by R. Vaughan Williams) and the Doxology emphasize this message. The exultation in the music, if not the words, speaks to children.

One family, who were not able to attend the funeral of an uncle in a distant city, planned a service for him and held it in their home at the same time his funeral was taking place. Years later the children spoke of how much this had meant to them.

Another family, who wanted their children to keep vivid the memories of their grandparents who had died, had the custom on special family occasions of showing their pictures and talking together about the good times they had had with them. Family movies help to keep these memories alive.

In times of grief, whenever possible we need to turn children's thoughts and feelings outward and help them to express their sorrow and love in some constructive way, perhaps by doing something that would please the one who has died or helping someone in the family who is also grieving. Ben's mother died when he was ten. They had been very close, and Ben was well aware that his frequent fights with a sister who irritated him had distressed his mother. When she died Ben knew what he could do for her. Then and there he decided that he would fight no more with this sister, and from that day on there were no more fights.

Sometimes even very young children surprise us by their desire and ability to help in times of sorrow. Five-year-old Bob (referred to in chapter 1) just prior to his father's death had been frightened in a school fire drill because he was hard of hearing and had not understood; each morning since, he had been putting up a fight when his mother took him to school. The Friday his father was buried, Bob put his arms around his mother and said, "Mommie, I can go to school Monday. The little things don't matter."

A wise minister, when he had to tell two young children that their mother had died, took them on his lap and with an arm around each he talked with them. Then he said, "Now you will need to help each other," and together they thought of some of the things their mother had done for them which they could do for each other.

Nine-year-old Edna was grieving over the loss of her grandmother, with whom she had spent many companionable hours. Her mother suggested that she write a story about Grandmother and their good times together. This proved to be a happy outlet for Edna and a loving tribute to her grandmother. As each chapter was finished, she read it to her family, and they all relived the good times and fun they had had with Grandmother.

A preschool teacher says that when one of the children tells her that a member of his family has died, she always asks the child to tell her about the happy times they had together.

The Sunday morning the children in the church school referred to earlier were told that their minister had died, the director of religious education asked the junior and junior high children if they would like to make a special memorial issue of their church school newspaper. Although the last issue of the year had just been completed with some difficulty because it was during their busy final weeks at their public schools, they eagerly accepted the suggestion, and no other issue had ever been worked on with such willing hearts and loving care.

Prayer can be an expression of love in times of grief. A five-year-old boy, after the death of a little friend, with no suggestion from his parents, prayed for several nights that God would comfort her family "because they will miss Joan so much." Children have warm hearts; it is natural for them to pray for those whom they love. And it will help them to continue to remember in their prayers the person they loved who has died.

One mother felt that her children had been helped after the death of their grandfather when at prayer time they remembered him in such a prayer as the following: "Dear God, bless our Grandfather. We thank you for him and for all the good times we had together. We do not know what his new life is like, but we know that it is good, for you have planned it."

The attitude of the parents in times of grief, as at all

times, is the most important influence in the home. Their feelings, both conscious and unconscious, are quickly sensed and assimilated by the children.

After the funeral of a daughter the burden of grief was lightened for another child in the family when the mother said, "What helped me most was the minister's prayer of thanksgiving that we had had her as long as we had." Thanksgiving and gratitude, essential in a good life, have healing power in times of grief. The Jewish memorial service is predominantly a service of praise to God and affirmation of his goodness.

C. S. Lewis, after the death of his wife, said that in his first days of mourning his thoughts were about himself, then about his wife and about God. He writes in *A Grief Observed:*

In that order. The order and the proportions exactly what they ought not to have been. And I see that I have nowhere fallen into that mode of thinking about either which we call praising them. Yet that would have been best for me. Praise is the mode of love which always has some element of joy in it. Praise in due order; of Him as the giver, of her as the gift. Don't we in praise somewhat enjoy what we praise, however far we are from it? . . . By praising I can still, in some degree, enjoy her, and already in some degree, enjoy Him.

It is good to praise God for the gift of our loved one who has died, and to pray that "increasing in knowledge and love of thee, he may go from strength to strength, in the life of perfect service." [1] Not only should we keep those who have died in our prayers, but it helps us to remember that they continue to love and pray for us.

Many people who have had a close and deep relationship with loved ones who have died are vividly aware at times of their spiritual presence. Elizabeth Gray Vining writes in *The World in Tune:* "There have been times . . . when I have been aware of the presence of one whom I loved and could not see. The joy of the moment and the lasting, vivid quality of the memory seem to speak for its authenticity."

Our beloved dead are now a part of that great company in heaven with whom we have fellowship— those we have loved in this world, others unknown in person but akin to us in spirit, and many more from countless generations. They are those referred to in the Bible as the "great cloud of witnesses" by whom we are surrounded. The "communion of saints" is real and very powerful.

[1] *Book of Common Prayer.*

4
EXPERIENCING LIFE AND DEATH WITH CHILDREN

The best way in which we can help prepare children to meet the mystery of death is to see to it that they are living rich, full lives here and now, and that they are using well the opportunities which life presents.

The Christian evangelist Kagawa once said if he had the religious education of a child in his care, he would give him as many experiences as possible in God's world of nature. To have a "direct relation to the universe" Emerson felt was the right of every child. What can a child learn from the natural world around him that will help him to grow in understanding, appreciation, and confidence, and thus not only enrich his life now but inspire him with trust in facing the end of life in this world?

Awareness of the beauty, majesty, and order in the universe awakens a consciousness of the greatness and the dependability of the Creator. Exploring the night sky can be such an experience. Children have always been fascinated by the sun, moon, and stars, and today's children, who are caught up in the wonder and excitement of man's exploration of outer space and his trips to the moon, are eager to learn more about the heavens.

An evening with a telescope, observing the vastness and the order of the universe above us, can be both fun and an expanding experience. Generally there is someone in the neighborhood who, if not a professional astronomer, studies the stars as a hobby and would be glad to share his telescope and en-enthusiasm with a group of children. Such a happening is likely to awaken in the children the same feeling that Sara Teasdale expressed in the last stanza of her poem "Stars."

> And I know that I
> Am honored to be
> Witness
> Of so much majesty.[1]

Visit a planetarium if one is near; if not, obtain an inexpensive sky chart. The chart will enable the children to recognize some of the stars and constellations and to become familiar with the changes in their positions which take place with the changing seasons. What keeps the stars from falling or bumping into each other, the children may wonder. This question will open the way for them to learn about the great invisible power of gravity which holds

[1] Reprinted with permission of The Macmillan Company from *Collected Poems* by Sara Teasdale. Copyright 1920 by The Macmillan Company, renewed 1948 by Mamie T. Wheless.

all things together and keeps the earth, the other planets, and all the stars moving in an orderly way; gravity is a power upon which we can depend.

Scientific books on stars written for children can be borrowed from a public library. The more the children do their own investigating and then sharing this knowledge with their family, the more meaningful it will be to them. The best role for adults is one of encouraging, listening, and enjoying the discoveries.

There are many activities which will involve the children, such as making transparencies by painting night scenes with outlines of trees and buildings, and pricking different sizes of holes in the sky for stars; these can then be placed in the window or in front of a lamp so the light can shine through "the stars." A ten-year-old, after studying the stars during his summer vacation, used his Christmas money for materials to construct his own telescope. In this family they made up a game about the stars similar to "twenty questions."

It can be a rewarding experience when families take time to watch the sunset. A boy felt that his most vivid awareness of the presence of God was one evening when he and his father watched a sunset and his father quoted "To a Waterfowl" by Bryant. Younger children after watching a sunset will appreciate George Macdonald's poem "The Sun Has Gone Down." (For the text of these poems see 'Resource Materials for Use with Children.")

After living in the presence of the sunset and the night sky, the children will understand how the ancient Hebrews felt as they looked up at the very same stars during the long nights on the hillside with their sheep, or watched the sunset from the roof of their home when the family came together at the end of the day's work. Though the sky uttered not a word, it spoke, and its message the Hebrews put into a beautiful poem in our Bible:

> The heavens proclaim God's splendor,
>   the sky speaks of his handiwork;
> day after day takes up the tale,
>   night after night makes him known;
> their speech has never a word,
>   not a sound for the ear,
> and yet their message spreads
>   the wide world over,
> their meaning carries to earth's end.
>   (Ps. 19:1-4 Moffatt)

Witnessing the beauty and grandeur of the heavens, we feel awe and wonder which leads us to worship; learning about the orderly movements of the stars and planets, we realize the dependability of the Creator, and we are inspired to trust.

Children are endowed by nature with curiosity, and they are eager to explore the world around them. As they discover the cycles in inanimate things they learn that nothing is permanently lost. Every child should have a magnifying glass; with it much which might be passed by unnoticed becomes fascinating. On a summer morning a child can go out early and through his glass observe the crystal-clear globe of a dewdrop. He can learn that, though it disappears at the touch of his finger or the warmth of the sun, it is not lost but is drawn up into the atmosphere to be again changed into water or frost or hail or snow. In winter through his glass he can study the varied and orderly designs of snowflakes. He will be interested in knowing about the first person to photograph snowflakes. (See "Suggested Activities.")

In planting and caring for a small garden or bulbs in a window, children experience something of the wonder of growing things and learn of the cycles in plant life.

Trees, readily accessible, can be an absorbing study for children. On an autumn walk in the park they will enjoy the colored leaves falling on the ground; they can learn how these will enrich the soil which feeds the trees, observe the tiny knots on the branch where the leaves had been which are now leaf buds that will grow into new leaves in the spring.

They will be surprised to know that in the land where Jesus lived there are olive trees living today which were there when Jesus was a boy, almost two thousand years ago, and that in California there are giant sequoia trees thought to be between three and four thousand years old—the oldest and largest living things in the world. They may like to keep a record book containing leaves of different trees and what they are finding out about them.

Experiences with living creatures, seeing birth, growth, change, and the ongoingness of life through change—help children develop attitudes of trust and confident expectation toward changes which are inherent in all life and toward that mysterious transition called death. They can watch a butterfly emerge from a cocoon and become aware of the exciting miracle of change. They will enjoy the stories, "What the Caterpillar Found Out" and "The Dragonfly Grubs." The poem "Over and Over Again," made from ideas given by a group of children, may inspire them to write about some of the wonders they are discovering. (See "Resource Materials for Use with Children.") We can relate some of the verses in the Bible to their experiences. "Stand still, think of the wonders of God." "This is the doing of the Eternal—we cannot but watch and wonder" (Job 37:14; Ps. 118:23 Moffatt).

Awareness of forces in nature which cannot be seen and invisible powers within ourselves will help children to be conscious of the reality of the unseen. They might think of all the forces in nature they cannot see but which they know are real because they see the results of their power—growth, gravity, electricity, wind. They can then think of the unseen powers within themselves—thoughts, memories, conscience, humor, love. A wise mother of three boys wrote:

We can do our children no better service than by helping them to appreciate this mysterious, unseen power of personality, whether in life around us or in biography. We shall find that the invisible forces of nature offer parables for us, as they did for Jesus. Remember how he used the wind to illustrate the work of God's Spirit. If we show our children how to play with the wind, magnets and electricity, their idea of reality can never be confined to the visible, and it will be easier for them to imagine an unseen world. We can even ask a little child, "Where is Daddy's love? Can you touch it? Can rain or cold spoil it? No, for it is not like the things that we see and touch, all of which get worn out in time. It will last forever." [2]

It is impossible to live richly without experiencing sorrow and suffering. Sorrowful experiences as well as happy ones are a part of life. Sorrow has something to teach us. To protect a child from all suffering, even if it were possible, would be to deny him a part of human experience, as well as be an inadequate preparation for later years. If children learn to handle "little sufferings" when they come, they will grow in understanding, compassion, and strength. Then they will be better prepared to face and live through the larger sufferings which at some time come to all of us.

When children experience sorrow, we help them best by acknowledging their feelings, letting them express their grief, and sharing it with them.

[2] *Problems of a Little Child*, by a Mother (Boston: Pilgrim Press, 1928), pp. 100-101.

Dr. Haim Ginott told of a mother saying to her child who was crying over a dead fish: "Do you know what your tears tell me? They tell me you are growing up; you can really feel, and feel deeply."

In a summer camp seven-year-old Mark, tramping through the woods with his group, accidentally stepped on and killed a baby rabbit. All the children were stunned and very distressed, especially Mark. The leader, holding the still little form in his hand, said that accidents happen in our world and we are sad. He spoke of God's love for all creatures and told them that Jesus had said not a sparrow is forgotten before God. It was suggested that they bury the rabbit and have a service for it. After the children had made the small grave ready, they all said the Twenty-Third Psalm, then the leader made a prayer and the children joined him in the Lord's Prayer. They had done what they could; they had given expression to their sorrow and their faith. Though it was a subdued group of children, they were now ready to move on and give themselves to the day's activities.

The death of a pet may cause a child acute suffering. Sometimes when a beloved dog dies, a parent, through the mistaken idea that he should always keep his child happy, immediately tries to replace it with another dog. The child may resent this; he wants the dog he has known and loved. His feelings need to be respected, and he should be allowed to grieve. A little girl for several months after her dog Red died would not touch another dog because Red, her faithful friend for seven years, had been unhappy if she petted another dog. The child who has lost a dog should be given another, but it is better not to do so immediately. A little later he will be ready to welcome with joy another puppy. The new pet will not take the place of the one that died; he will have his own place, and the child will find that his heart is large enough to love both.

A child is often helped in his grief by planning a simple service for the burial of his pet. Such a ceremony has several values: it helps the child to accept the finality of his pet's death, the loving tribute provides an outlet for his feelings, and it can be an expression of his faith in the love of God.

Above all it is the experience of love—being loved and giving love—which enables children to live happy, outgoing lives. And it is knowing unselfish, forgiving love that is the best preparation for meeting whatever the future years will bring and for facing the fact of death with trust.

Children who are part of a family in which there is deep affection, appreciation for all life, and dedication to service build a foundation upon which to stand in meeting all the exigencies of life. When the home fails in this quality of living, then relatives, friends, and the church or synagogue need to see that they provide enriching, challenging experiences and understanding, sustaining relationships upon which the children can rely.

Opportunities can be made for children to have

firsthand, personal contact with dedicated people who are giving themselves in service in today's world. Children are interested in other people, and through stories and biography they can come to know great men and women of the past and present who have taken it upon themselves to help alleviate some of the needs in our world. A man whose life is dedicated to working for understanding and peace in the world was asked what led him to give his life in this work. Quickly he replied, "It was reading the stories of people who gave their lives in service in the books I borrowed from our church school library."

We need to help children in outgoing love and concern. Opportunities for such growth confront them daily in their home, at school, and on the playground. Children are quick to respond to the troubles and needs of other children. A group of seven-year-old Negro children in an inner city church heard about an American Indian boy who had been seriously hurt in a school accident. Spontoneously they said, "Let's write him a letter. Let's draw some pictures for him." And that afternoon their colored pictures and the following letter, signed by six children, were sent across the country to a child they had never seen:

> Dear Louis:
> We are sorry you are hurt and in the hospital. We are sorry. We will be glad when you are out. We love you.

We can broaden the circle of children's relationships by seeing that they have friends with different ethnic and cultural backgrounds. Some families invite a child from a different background to spend part of the summer vacation with them. Such an experience can have far-reaching significance for both the visiting child and the host family.

Children can be introduced to causes which will challenge them to do their part in helping to make this world a better place for all. Since some children are very sensitive to the suffering of others, the emphasis should be placed on the positive—what people have done to help, what is now being done, and what can be done. Ida Tarbell said her interest in working for peace in our world began when as a young child she gave her pennies to help the victims of war. Not infrequently, as early as at seven years a child has become aware of some need in the world and formed a purpose to help when he grows up. Jane Addams was not quite seven when with her father she visited a tenement district and saw the sad condition of the city's poor. She then made the surprising statement, "When I grow up I'm going to have a big house, but I'm not going to build it among the other big houses. I'm going to build it right in the midst of horrid little houses like these."

The larger family circle of the church should be a fellowship of the concerned, where children are nurtured in a life of redemptive love and are challenged to a life of commitment.

To know this quality of living in others and within ourselves enables us to believe that Love is at the heart of the universe; a stream cannot rise higher than its source. If in Love "we live and move and have our being," then death and all the other great mysteries which we do not now understand can be entrusted to him who planned the whole.[3]

[3] See "Suggested Activities" for further enriching experiences.

5

CLARIFYING OUR OWN THINKING ABOUT DEATH

"If a man die, shall he live again?" (Job 14:14*a*) is the oldest and the most universal question men have asked. A hunger for life beyond death is instinctive, and in all cultures mankind has shown a deep, intuitive belief in a life beyond the death of his physical body.

Even our most primitive ancestors believed that man lived in some form after death. They had a very earthy concept of the hereafter, as is shown by their burying weapons and food in the graves of their warriors to provide for their needs in the "Happy Hunting Ground." As man evolved, he came to realize that there was in him a spirit which was different from his material body; then he began to think of the life beyond in spiritual terms. Lecomte du Noüy, the physicist and Nobel Prize winner, bears witness to the reality of the spiritual world: "The destiny of Man is not limited to his existence on earth."

Death is in the order of creation as truly as birth is in the divine plan. The first stage of life as we know it is the babe in his envelope within his mother. Here he is secure and warm and asleep; he is unaware of anyone else. While in this somnolent life he is developing a body with eyes, ears, a brain, which he will need in his next stage of existence.

When this body is sufficiently developed, he undergoes a traumatic experience. He is impelled to leave his home; he suffers a transition generally accompanied by great struggle. If the baby could think, this expulsion would no doubt seem like death to him, for he leaves the only home he has known for the unknown.

His response to his next stage of existence is a cry, but soon he is exploring an exciting new life. In this life he becomes aware of others—others who give him love and meet his needs. He has need now for the body he has been developing, and through using it and relating to others he grows and develops.

In this second life, through his freedom and his ability to think, choose, and act, he has the opportunity to develop qualities of the spirit—faith, love, courage, endurance, and patience. This spiritual body which he can build he will take with him when he leaves his physical body. In his next life he will use and develop further his spiritual self.

To those who value life in this world and use its opportunities to grow, to love, and to serve, it should seem reasonable to think of death as a transition into a still larger life—a life with greater possibilities for fulfillment, love, and work. "The birth of a human being is pregnant with meaning, why not death?" asks Carl Jung.

The worst of death is the fear of death. The writer to the Hebrews spoke of "those who through fear of death were subject to lifelong bondage" (2:15) . What is the basis for the fear of death? Anticipation of suffering, loneliness, dread of separation, judgment, fear of the unknown, of ceasing to be?

The testimony of doctors, ministers, and those who have been with their loved ones at the time of death seems to belie most of these fears. If there is pain it is generally before death, not at the actual time of death. Most deaths are peaceful. If there has been fear of death, the fear seems to leave the person when he comes to the experience of dying. It is replaced by a calm acceptance, and sometimes there is a surprised expression of elation which seems to indicate some new awareness of the meaning of death. An elderly woman who was dying said to her nurse when she tried to give her nourishment, "I am going through an interesting transition and I do not want to be disturbed." There are accounts of the dying apparently seeing and responding to loved ones who had died and are now present to them. At the time of death many seem to be conscious of two worlds, the world they are leaving and a spiritual dimension not visible to those standing by.

In every age there have been those who have looked forward with confident anticipation to the experiences beyond death.

Socrates, before he drank the hemlock, was asked by his friend Crito how he wanted to be buried. With some humor Socrates replied, "However you please. If you can catch me . . . I shall go away to the joys of the blessed." Then he assured his grieving friends about the death of his body with the words:

The spirit is not there. Is it not strange, my friends, that after all I have said to convince you I am going to the society of the happy, you still think this body to be Socrates? Bury my body where you please, but do not mourn over it as if it were Socrates. Wherefore be of good cheer about death and know of a certainty that no evil can happen to a good man in life or in death.

All the great religions have believed in a life beyond death, and in the relationship between the quality of our living here and our place in the life thereafter.

Taoism says:

Life is a going forth. Death is a returning home. The bow-sheath is slipped off; the clothes-bag is dropped;
   and in the confusion the soul wings its flight
     on the great journey home.[1]

Buddhism makes clear the importance of righteous living here as a condition of happiness in the hereafter:

[1] Robert E. Hume, *Treasure-House of the Living Religions* (New York: Charles Scribner's Sons, 1932), p. 73.

That individual in this world who reflecteth right
    thoughts,
Who uttereth right words, who doeth right acts,
Who is learned and virtuous here in this brief life—
    He, after the dissolution of his body, goeth to heaven.[2]

The Jewish writer in Ecclesiastes says, "He [God]
has put eternity into man's mind" (3:11). And the
book of Wisdom of Solomon states:

> God created man for immortality,
> And made him the image of his own eternity.
>   (2:23 Goodspeed)

The first century A.D. was a time of great spiritual
hunger. Many were searching for meaning in their
lives; they were asking ultimate questions and were
open to values beyond the temporal. These were the
people who responded to the good news of Jesus Christ
who, as Paul wrote to young Timothy, had "complete-
ly abolished death, and has now, through the Gospel,
opened to us men the shining possibilities of the life
that is eternal" (II Tim. 1:10 Philips). They em-
braced this new faith, found meaning for their lives
and the power to live triumphantly in the midst of
uncertainty and tragedy. When they faced persecution
for their faith and suffered death itself, as many did,
they were able to meet it with confidence, for they
had found the life which is immortal.

[2] *Ibid.,* p. 65.

While Christianity, with all the great religions, believes that there is a spirit in man which lives beyond
the death of his physical body, its emphasis it not on
existence after death; its concern is eternal life. Eternal life is more than continuance of existence; it is
no less than the life of God dwelling in us. This is the
great promise of the Christian faith. It was for this
purpose that Christ came into the world—that men
might have life which is eternal. "I came that they
may have life, and have it abundantly" (John
10:10b).

When Jesus was asked how eternal life could be
obtained, he said it consisted in keeping the two
great commandments: "You shall love the Lord your
God with all your heart, and with all your soul, and
with all your strength, and with all your mind; and
your neighbor as yourself. . . . Do this and you will
live" (Luke 10:27-28; Matt. 22:37-39).

Jesus lived on earth this life which is eternal; he
incarnated the self-giving, creative life of love. And
to those who would hear he said: "I am the way, and
the truth, and the life" (John 14:6).

Eternal life is a life of love, and it begins here and
now. When we have within us qualities which are
immortal, indestructible, we become immortal. "We
know that we have passed out of death into life, because we love the brethren. He who does not love
remains in death" (I John 3:14).

There are degrees of life. This eternal life, which
those who love now possess, can grow in increasing

fullness during the immediate days and years ahead, and beyond the gates of time. "We are God's children now; it does not yet appear what we shall be, but we know that when he appears we shall be like him, for we shall see him as he is" (I John 3:2).

In times of grief Christians have always been comforted by Jesus' promise to his disciples on his last night with them; knowing that he would die on the morrow he said: "Let not your hearts be troubled; believe in God, believe also in me. In my Father's house are many rooms; if it were not so, would I have told you that I go to prepare a place for you? And when I go and prepare a place for you, I will come again and will take you to myself, that where I am you may be also" (John 14:1-3).

After the crucifixion, his resurrection appearances convinced his friends beyond doubt that he was their living Lord who could, as he promised, be with them always. It was this knowledge that changed his disciples from frightened, discouraged men into the courageous, joyful apostles who went into a hostile world fearlessly proclaiming that Jesus who had been crucified was Lord over life and over death. When they were put in prison and commanded to preach no more in the name of Jesus, they replied: "We cannot but speak of what we have seen and heard" (Acts 4:20).

To those who have followed the studies of eminent investigators in the field of parapsychology, the accounts in the Bible of supernatural appearances, warnings, and guidance no longer seem miraculous in the sense of being contrary to law, but seem to be phenomena involving higher laws than we now understand. Those who are open to such insights are inclined to give credence to Frederic Myers' prophecy that the time will come when it will be impossible to doubt the appearances of Jesus to his friends after his death.

To the disciples death was only an incident in the eternal life they had already begun to live. Saul, the persecutor of Christians who, after his vision of the risen Christ, became Paul the apostle to the Gentiles, wrote from prison shortly before his execution, "For me to live is Christ, and to die is gain" (Phil. 1:21).

Down through the ages, Christians have been able to face death with calm assurance. A minister who knew that soon he was to die sent an Easter message to the children of his church. In it he quoted a poem which he had used with his young people when he discussed the mystery of death:

> We wake each morn as if the Maker's grace
> Did us afresh from nothingness derive,
>   That we might sing, "How happy is our case,
>   How beautiful it is to be alive!" . . .
> And ever toward new heights we still may strive,
> Till, just as any other friend's, we press
> Death's hand:
>   And, having died, feel none the less,
>   How beautiful it is to be alive!

The author in her early twenties wrote the following poem. Now that she has reached her "threescore years and ten" she looks forward with greater interest and anticipation to this nearer adventure.

The Greater Adventure

Swing wide, O Door that men call Death,
I've lived my threescore years and ten,
Years interwoven—the good, the bad,
The failure and success,
A fall, a new start, till the next fall:
Then begin again.
Shall I repine?
Nay, know the God of life,
Mightier his love than our sin,
Greater his strength than our weakness.
He who has given the years that have gone
Has other work for man to do.
So swing wide, O Door that men call Death,
For death thou art not, but life to me!

6

CONFRONTING THE WHY OF TRAGIC DEATHS

In the midst of living there suddenly may be tragic, meaningless death. How can we answer the *why* when death is caused by catastrophes of nature, by man's folly, sin, and war?

A kindergarten boy and girl were overheard discussing a recent hurricane: "God sent the hurricane and the hurricane is no good," stated the girl. The boy would not agree that God had sent the hurricane. "But," he stoutly maintained, "God stands by."

There is much that we do not undesrtand about this universe. It appears that it is still unfinished; like man, it is in the process of becoming. Paul speaks of the created order and man as interdependent, straining toward a new birth. He writes of a cosmic redemption: "We know that the whole creation has been groaning in travail together until now; and not only the creation, but we ourselves, who have the first fruits of the Spirit, groan inwardly as we wait for adoption as sons" (Rom. 8:22-23) .

The unfinished universe confronts man with a challenge. And through responding to this challenge men have grown in knowledge and in capability. Children are interested in learning how through understanding of the laws of nature we are discovering ways to prevent many catastrophes. We know now that we must not cut down all the trees on a mountainside, for the trees absorb and hold back water when it rains, and thus prevent it from rushing down the mountain causing floods that destroy homes. Today we have a net of weather stations, some as far away as our satellites, which make it possible to predict weather far in advance and thus prevent or mitigate effects of many catastrophes. There is much in our world, it appears, that God has left for man to do.

What of the tragic deaths caused by people's carelessness, indifference, and inhumanity? What of the horrors of war? "Why?" is a question with which mankind has always had to wrestle. Unfortunately we sometimes hear good people give the unworthy answer, "It is God's will." [1] God does not will tragedy and suffering; it would be contrary to the nature of a God of love. Let us never blame God for man's sin, carelessness, and ignorance.

God is more sorry than we are when tragedies happen; he is always there to help us in and through sorrow and suffering. God is able to deal with tragedy. From all ages there are illustrations of people who suffered great disasters and, in the end, led triumphant lives.

[1] Recommended for further reading: *The Will of God,* by Leslie Weatherhead (Nashville: Abingdon Press, 1944).

An inspiring present-day example is the story of Iona Henry. In the spring of 1952 tragedy wiped out Mrs. Henry's entire family. Her fourteen-year-old daughter died of cancer. A month later on a motor trip to visit her husband's minister-father there was an accident in which her husband and her ten-year-old son were killed. Iona Henry, near death from terrible injuries, regained consciousness in a hospital where she learned of the death of her husband and son. She had no wish to live. What enabled her to make the pain-filled, lonely struggle? After months of bitter discouragement she wrote of "the last high hill" she climbed one Easter season as she sat in the chapel of the college where she was teaching English:

Suddenly . . . I saw it clearly. . . . The answer was this: Whatever is, is: you cannot change it. Whatever has happened, *has* happened, and you cannot go back and change any of it, however or whyever it happened. The question is not "Why did it happen?" but "What do I do *now?*" Sit and fight it, all the rest of my life? Sit and rebel and gnash my teeth? That will not help at all. The thing to do, wherever I am, is to do the very best I can and to leave the rest to God. . . . What must be done may seem impossible, but God has a way of working out the impossible. Do your part; do what must be done *and do it well.*

It was so clear! It was not a case of what I wanted to do but of what, with God's help, I had to do. I had wanted to shut myself up in the little house that my selfishness had built, and die. "Move out of it," said God. "Go to work and improve your skills. You can sing the Lord's song in a strange land, if you want to." [2]

Mrs. Henry did just that. She went back to college, got her M.A., later her doctorate, and became a professor of English. Today she is an inspiration to all who know her or hear about her. (See "From a Letter" in "Enriching Materials for Adults.")

When our children face a tragedy and ask, "Why did God let it happen?" what can we say to them? We can help them to understand that the words "God created man in his own image" mean that God gave us the freedom to choose and to create. Sometimes our decisions are not wise. Sometimes the driver of a car drives too fast or makes an unwise decision and causes a serious accident. And since man has this freedom to make choices, he can, if he chooses, use these God-given powers to do evil instead of good, and thereby cause death and great suffering. We see this especially in times of war; war is the opposite of God's will.

Why did God give this power to men if they can cause such terrible suffering? "Why," asked an eleven-year-old, "does God not make people be good, instead of letting everyone choose and make mistakes?" We can help children to see that if we did not have free-

[2] *Triumph Over Tragedy*, Iona Henry with Frank Mead (Westwood, N. J.: Fleming H. Revell, 1957), pp. 114-15. Used with permission of the author, Mrs. John H. McLaughlin.

dom of choice we would be like puppets. It is only
through choosing what is right, overcoming tempta-
tions, and doing the things which often are very hard
that we grow in goodness and courage and become
strong persons of worth, the kind of people who are
able to make our world a better place in which to live.
God showed great faith in us when he gave us this
freedom to choose. The good must be worth the risk.
Through the right use of our freedom we have the
opportunity to grow and to become worthy sons and
daughters of God.

After we have said all this, we are still unsatisfied.
When the full extent of "man's inhumanity to man"
impinges upon us, we realize that there are some
questions we cannot answer; reason alone cannot explain them. Ultimately the answers lie in the in-
finities, and we are finite. We "see through a glass
darkly." We and our children need to acknowledge
and accept our limitations.

Jesus did not explain the *why* of evil; he defeated it.
Throughout his life and in his death he taught and
demonstrated a way of overcoming evil. In the cross
of Christ we see unmerited suffering transformed
through redemptive love into victory and saving
grace. To his disciples, Jesus said, "In the world you
have tribulation, but be of good cheer, I have overcome the world" (John 16:33*b*).

In the end we have to make a leap of faith and
trust the God who revealed himself in Jesus Christ.
Faith is necessary in all areas of life. Science makes a

venture of faith when it frames a hypothesis. A president of the Massachusetts Institute of Technology said, "Science is grounded in faith just as is religion, and scientific truth, like religious truth, consists of hypotheses, never wholly verified, that fit the facts more or less closely." [3] We realize how necessary faith is in human relationships. Surely in our relationship with the Highest, whose "thoughts are not our thoughts," we can understand the immense need for faith.

Lady Julian of Norwich, the first English woman of letters, struggled for thirteen years to reconcile the sin and suffering in the world with the love of God. "Why," she asked, "had God permitted sin to come into the world?" She was living as an anchoress in Norwich Cathedral, praying and ministering to the people who came to her for help when, in her thirtieth year, she had a revelation. On a May morning in the year 1373 she was taught, she said, all that she needed to know. She writes:

Jesus in this vision informed me . . . "Sin must needs be, but all shall be well. All shall be well; and all manner of things shall be well." . . .

In these words I saw a high marvellous secret hid in God—a secret which he shall truly openly make known to us in heaven. In this knowing we shall truly see the

[3] Harry Emerson Fosdick, *The Assurance of Immortality* (New York: The Macmillan Company, 1918), p. 103.

cause why he permitted sin to come. And in this knowing
we shall have endless joy.[4]

Lady Julian questioned God's love no more, but
carried on her work of prayer and service for forty
more years with the joyful faith that love was God's
purpose and would prevail.

Children have an instinctive faith; it is natural for
them to believe. The questions a child asks are open
doors, invitations to enter his mind and heart. They
present us with opportunities to undergird his faith
with beliefs which will satisfy his maturing mind and
to enlarge his heart through guiding him in understanding relationships. If children can see that life
with all its pain and difficulties has purpose, and that
God has entrusted us with a crucial part in achieving
that purpose; if they can see God working in and
through men of good will to overcome the tragedies
that are the consequences of man's sin and to make
a better and a more peaceful world; then while the
mystery of sin, suffering, and death remains, it will be
a mystery shot through with light. They can then
wholeheartedly accept the challenges which life presents and become active participants in helping to
build a just and humane world where brotherhood
shall prevail.

When we give ourselves to the fulfillment of God's
will and become channels for his Spirit, we know the

[4] *The Revelation of Divine Love of Julian of Norwich,* trans. by
James Walsh (New York: Harper & Row, 1961), pp. 91, 92.

meaning of fellowship with God, with the "communion of saints," and with all men of good will.
Then we become able to say with Paul: "I am sure
that neither death, nor life, nor angels, nor princi-
palities, nor things present, nor things to come, nor
powers, nor height, nor depth, nor anything else
in all creation, will be able to separate us from the
love of God in Christ Jesus our Lord" (Rom. 8:38-
39).

RESOURCE MATERIALS
FOR USE WITH
CHILDREN

VERSES FROM THE BIBLE

In the beginning God created the heavens and the earth.
—Genesis 1:1

God created man . . . and blessed them.—Genesis 1:27*a*, 28

The earth is the Lord's and the fullness thereof,
the world and those who dwell therein.—Psalm 24:1

O Lord, how manifold are thy works!
In wisdom hast thou made them all.—Psalm 104:24

O give thanks to the Lord, for he is good,
for his steadfast love endures for ever. . . .
To him who made the great lights, . . .
the sun to rule over the day, . . .
the moon and stars to rule over the night, . . .
O give thanks to the God of heaven,
for his steadfast love endures for ever.—Psalm 136:1,
7, 8, 9, 26

Stand still,
Think of the wonders of God.—Job 37:14 (Moffatt)

God . . . does great things which we cannot comprehend.
—Job 37:5*b*

O Lord my God, thou art very great!—Psalm 104:1

This is the doing of the Eternal—
   we can but watch and wonder.—Psalm 118:23
   (Moffatt)

While the earth remains,
seedtime and harvest,
cold and heat,
summer and winter,
day and night, shall not cease.—Genesis 8:22

He has made everything beautiful in its time.—Ecclesiastes 3:11a

For lo, the winter is past,
   the rain is over and gone.
The flowers appear on the earth,
   the time of singing has come—Song of Solomon 2:11-
   12a

This is the day which the Lord has made;
   let us rejoice and be glad in it.—Psalm 118:24

O sing to the Lord a new song,
   for he has done marvelous things!—Psalm 98:1

Let everything that breathes praise the Lord!
   Praise the Lord!—Psalm 150:6

How precious to me are thy thoughts, O God!
   How vast is the sum of them!
If I would count them, they are more than the sand.
   When I awake, I am still with thee.—Psalm 139:17-18

The Lord hears when I call to him.—Psalm 4:3b

For thou, O Lord, art good and forgiving,
   abounding in steadfast love to all who call on thee. . . .

In the day of my trouble I call on thee,
 for thou dost answer me. . . .
Teach me thy way, O Lord,
 that I may walk in thy truth. . . .
I give thanks to thee, O Lord my God, with my whole
     heart,
 and I will glorify thy name for ever.—Psalm 86:5, 7,
     11, 12

The Lord is my shepherd, I shall not want.—Psalm 23:1

Jesus said: "This is my commandment, that you love one
 another as I have loved you. . . . You are my friends if
 you do what I command you.
 "By this all men will know that you are my disciples,
if you have love one for another."—John 15:12, 14; 13:35

For we are the temple of the living God, as God said,
 "I will live in them and move among them,
 and I will be their God,
 and they will be my people. . . .
 And I will be a father to you,
 and you shall be my sons and daughters,
 says the Lord Almighty."—II Corinthians 6:16b, 18

We are fellow workmen for God—I Corinthians 3:9a

Be doers of the word, and not hearers only—James 1:22

Be kind to one another, tenderhearted, forgiving one
 another.—Ephesians 4:32

Let us love one another; for love is of God, and he who
 loves . . . knows God. . . . for God is love.—I John 4:7,
 8b

POEMS

Stars [1]

Alone in the night
On a dark hill
With pines around me
Spicy and still,

And a heaven full of stars
Over my head,
White and topaz
And misty red;

Myriads with beating
Hearts of fire
That aeons
Cannot vex or tire;

Up the dome of heaven
Like a great hill,
I watch them marching
Stately and still,

And I know that I
Am honored to be
Witness
Of so much majesty.

Sara Teasdale

From To a Waterfowl

Whither, midst falling dew,
While glow the heavens with the last steps of day,
Far, through their rosy depths, dost thou pursue
    Thy solitary way? . . .

There is a Power whose care
Teaches thy way along that pathless coast—
The desert and illimitable air—
    Lone wandering, but not lost. . . .

Thou'rt gone, the abyss of heaven
Hath swallowed up thy form; yet, on my heart
Deeply hath sunk the lesson thou hast given,
    And shall not soon depart.

He who, from zone to zone,
Guides through the boundless sky thy certain flight,
In the long way that I must tread alone,
    Will lead my steps aright.

William Cullen Bryant

The Miracle

Yesterday the twig was brown and bare;
Today the glint of green is there;
Tomorrow will be leaflets spare;
I know no thing so wondrous fair,
No miracle so strangely rare.
I wonder what will next be there!

L. H. Bailey

The Sun Is Gone Down

The sun is gone down
  And the moon's in the sky;
But the sun will come up,
  And the moon be laid by.

The flower is asleep,
  But it is not dead;
When the morning shines
  It will lift up its head.

When winter comes
  It will die—no, no!
It will only hide
  From the frost and the snow.

Sure is the summer,
  Sure is the sun,
The night and the winter
  Are shadows that run. . . .

The night and the winter
  Are shadows that run.

George Macdonald

The Snowflake [2]

Before I melt,
Come, look at me!
This lovely icy filigree!
Of a great forest
In one night
I make a wilderness
Of white:
By skyey cold
Of crystals made,
All softly, on
Your finger laid,
I pause, that you
My beauty see:
Breathe, and I vanish
Instantly.

Walter de la Mare

The Wind

Who has seen the wind?
  Neither I nor you.
But when the leaves hang trembling,
The wind is passing through.
Who has seen the wind?
  Neither you nor I.
But when the trees bow down their heads,
  The wind is passing by.

Christina Rossetti

[2] Reprinted by permission of the Literary Trustees of Walter de la Mare and The Society of Authors as their representative.

Over and Over Again [3]

Over and over again
The seed makes the plant,
And the plant bears fruit,
And the fruit drops seed,
And the seed makes the plant,—
Over and over again:
It never begins, and it never ends,
Nothing is old, and nothing is new,
And nothing is ever lost.

Over and over again
The soil feeds the tree,
And the tree drops its leaves,
And the leaves make soil,
And the soil feeds the tree,—
Over and over again:
It never begins, and it never ends,
Nothing is old, and nothing is new,
And nothing is ever lost.

Over and over again
The clouds drop rain,
And the air takes it back,
And it forms into clouds,
And the clouds drop rain,—
Over and over again:
It never begins, and it never ends,
Nothing is old, and nothing is new,
And nothing is ever lost.

Jeanette Perkins Brown

[3] Reprinted by permission of the estate of Jeanette Perkins Brown.

Caterpillar, Caterpillar [4]

Caterpillar, caterpillar, crawling on the ground,
Who has shown you where the leaves for your food are
found?

Caterpillar, caterpillar, growing as you feed,
Tell me how you know when you have eaten all you need.

Caterpillar, caterpillar, spinning in the air,
Whence came all those silken threads you are winding
there?

Caterpillar, caterpillar, how I wonder how
You could make the cradle snug where you're sleeping
now!

Caterpillar, caterpillar, what is telling you
As the days and weeks go by, when your sleep is through?

Caterpillar, caterpillar, I can feel you stir,
Pushing, breaking through the cradle where you were!

Caterpillar, caterpillar, crawling, sure and slow,
Out into the world again, *what has changed you so?*

Lovely, lovely creature, with your shining wings—
Caterpillar! You have filled me full of wonderings!

Jeanette Perkins Brown

[4] From *More Children's Worship in the Church School* by Jeanette Perkins Brown. Copyright, 1938 by Harper & Row, Publishers. Reprinted by permission of Harper & Row, Publishers.

From a Seed [5]

A tiny brown apple-seed
   Started to grow—
A shoot from above—
   A shoot down below.

Out spread the roots,
   Deep in the ground.
Up grew the stem—
   Tall, strong and round.

The years will roll by.
   The brown seed will be
A fruit-laden, spreading,
   Bright apple-tree!

What wonders does God
   Perform with a seed—
From seed to a tree
   Is wonder indeed!

Ilo Orleans

[5] Printed by permission from *This Wonderful Day: Poems of Prayer and Thanksgiving* by Ilo Orleans, published by the Union of American Hebrew Congregations, New York. Copyright 1958 by Ilo Orleans.

Easter Surprises [6]

Out of an egg comes a singing bird;
Out of a seed comes a flower;
Dark of the night turns to morning light;
Clouds turn to snow or to shower.
Look for the wonders of Easter-time,
Wonders that April will bring.
Open your eyes for a new surprise!
God is at work in the spring.

Edith Lovell Thomas

I Cannot See God

I cannot see God when I look,
  But still I know he's there,
I feel his sunshine on my face,
  His wind blows in my hair,
I cannot see God when I look,
  But still I know he's there,
In goodness, beauty and in love
  I find him everywhere.

Author Unknown

[6] From *The Whole World Singing,* compiled by Edith Lovell
Thomas. Friendship Press, New York. Copyright 1950.

God's Love [7]

We do not see the wind,
  We only hear it sigh;
It makes the grasses bend
  Whenever it goes by.

We do not see God's love,
  But we can feel it there
When friends, by word or deed,
  Are showing how they care.

We do not need to see
  To know the wind is here;
We do not need to see
  To know God's love is near.

Elizabeth Cushing Taylor

For the Things That Are Always [8]

O God, whose laws will never change,
We thank you for these things we know;
That after rain the sun will shine,
That after darkness, light appears,
That winter always brings the spring,
That after sleep, we wake again,
That life goes on, and love remains,
And life and love can never die.

Jeanette Perkins Brown

[7] By permission of the author.
[8] From *Pilgrim Elementary Teacher,* The Pilgrim Press.

Praise to God [9]

Praise be to God! There comes
  Out of the night the day,
Out of the gloom of wintertime
  Spring with its flowers gay.

Praise be to God! There comes
  Out of the chrysalis dry,
Yellow or blue or snowy winged
Gay little butterfly.

Praise be to God! There comes
  Out of the buried grain
Wonderful life, a hundredfold,
  Harvest of joy again.

Praise be to our Father, God!
  Giver of life to all,
Wonderful life that cannot die
  Given to great and small.

Alice M. Pullen

[9] By permission of the author.

STORIES ABOUT CHANGE AND CONTINUING LIFE IN NATURE

The Brown Bulbs' Secret [1]

One fall day, many weeks ago, the postman had brought a white envelope with Bill's name on it. Inside was a letter from Grandmother, which said:

Dear Bill,

    I am sending you a box of secrets. When you open the box, take good care of what you find. Then watch and wait.

                  Love, Grandmother

The next day, just when Bill thought he couldn't wait another minute, the postman came again. This time, sure enough, he brought a box from Grandmother.

When Bill opened the box he didn't know what to think. He was even a little disappointed, for all he saw were some little brown bulbs. "They don't look like very good secrets to me," Bill said.

"Oh," said Mother, "I think the bulbs hold the secrets inside themselves. Don't you remember what Grandmother's letter said?"

[1] Used by permission of the author, Mary E. Venable.

96

They read again: "Take good care of what you find. Then watch and wait."

Bill said, "I don't know how to take care of bulbs."

"I'll help you," Mother said.

It was fun, then, sifting some dirt from the garden until it was very soft, and filling a big pot with it, they buried the bulbs down, deep inside, and placed the pot in their sunniest window.

All this had been long ago in the fall. Now warmer days had come. Most of the snow had melted from the ground outside.

One day when he went to the window to water his bulbs, he saw something new. There, just peeping out of the soil, were tiny green leaves! Bill knew that at last his bulbs were beginning to tell their secret. Little green plants were slowly pushing up into the light.

Every day after that, Bill thought he could see that his plants had grown a little bit. He learned their name. They were called hyacinths.

Weeks passed. The hyacinths had grown quite large when some buds appeared. At first the tiny buds were covered in little green jackets. Bill kept asking what color the blossoms would show. "Watch and wait," Mother reminded him. "That is part of the secret."

At last the hyacinths bloomed. There they stood, tall and fragrant in the sunlight, proudly holding their bright pink flowers.

"Now," said Mother quietly, "we can *see* the secret that the brown bulbs held."

Bill looked at the bright blossoms, and thought of the little brown bulbs. "Mother," he said, "how can these flowers grow from little bulbs?"

"It is the life in the bulb that makes it grow, Bill," Mother answered. "You learned something about it while you were helping your plants to grow. You will learn more. But it is such a wonderful secret that no one understands all about it.

"God must be very wise and loving, to plan a world in which we find such wonderful secrets."

Bill was very quiet for a minute, enjoying a happy, wonderful feeling that was inside him.

Then he said, "Mother, I think I'll take my hyacinths to church school on Easter Day, so all the children can see them."

And that is what he did.

What the Caterpillar Found Out [2]

A caterpillar watched a beautiful butterfly flutter down to a cabbage leaf in the garden. "It must be the most wonderful thing in the world to be able to fly!" sighed the caterpillar as she crawled by. Then she stopped, for the butterfly was speaking to her.

"O kind caterpillar," she heard the butterfly say, "I am faint; I fear I am dying. Take care of my baby butterflies when they come to life." And with these words the butterfly folded her wings and died; and the caterpillar saw ten little round green eggs on the cabbage leaf.

"Poor, foolish butterfly to lay her eggs on a cabbage leaf and to ask me to be a nurse to her children," said the caterpillar. "And whatever shall I do? I cannot get the early dew and honey from the flowers which baby

[2] From *Pilgrim Elementary Teacher,* The Pilgrim Press. Adapted from "A Lesson in Faith" in *Parables from Nature* by Mrs. Alfred Gatty.

butterflies will need to grow strong and healthy, and much they will mind a crawling creature like me with their young wings carrying them over my head." She crawled round and round the butterfly's eggs to keep them safe and wondered what she would do.

At last she said to herself, "I will consult my friend the lark. He flies up into the sky so high he must be very wise." So the caterpillar sent a message to the lark, begging him to come to her, and she told him all her troubles.

"Do not worry, friend caterpillar," said the lark, "cabbage leaves which you eat yourself are the only food they will need, for the butterfly's babies will be little caterpillars like yourself."

"You are teasing me," said the caterpillar. "How could butterfly eggs turn into caterpillars?"

"I know something more wonderful than that," replied the lark. "Why, caterpillar, some day you will be a butterfly yourself."

"I thought you were wise and kind," said the caterpillar, "but you are neither. If you were wise you would not say that caterpillars came out of butterflies' eggs, and it is not kind to make fun of a crawling creature like me by telling me that some day I shall be a butterfly."

"Wait and see," sang the lark, and he flew up into the sky.

As the caterpillar watched him disappear into the blue she sighed and thought, "To fly must be the most wonderful thing in the world." Then round and round the butterfly eggs she crawled and worried about what she would do.

By and by on the cabbage leaf where the butterfly had laid her eggs she saw ten little green, fuzzy caterpillars.

"It's true," she cried, "caterpillars come from butterflies' eggs!" Then she remembered the second wonder the lark had told—that she, herself, would one day be a butterfly.

"I believe him," cried the caterpillar. "I have seen caterpillars come from a butterfly's eggs and greater wonders can be true. Some day I shall be able to fly!"

She hastened to tell the good news to all the caterpillars she knew. "Some day you will be butterflies! You will be able to fly!" she cried. But they laughed at her and said, "How can crawling creatures like us become butterflies?"

"I don't know," replied the caterpillar, "the wise, kind lark told me. But I have seen a butterfly's eggs turn into caterpillars and I believe greater wonders can be."

And when the wind blew cold and the leaves turned brown and the caterpillar felt herself grow sleepy she was not afraid. She said, "I will spin myself a warm blanket and go to sleep, and it may be that when I awake the wonder will have happened and I shall be a butterfly." So, fastened to a twig of a tree, she wound round and round herself a silken cover. And when the wind blew high and rocked all the branches of the tree and the snow covered the ground the caterpillar slept in her warm bed and dreamed of the days when she would fly.

All through the long, cold winter she slept. And when the warm spring came the sunbeams called to her, "It's time to wake up. The world is warm again and beautiful. Wake up!"

The caterpillar turned in her bed; she pushed her head out of her covers and looked about. The tree which had been all brown when she went to sleep was covered with tiny, green leaves. She pushed farther and farther out of her bed to see more of this beautiful, new world. It was all so different—the green grass had come back, and the flowers, and she heard the birds, who had disappeared, singing over her head. She felt different herself. Then she looked at herself.

"I am a butterfly!" she cried, and she spread the two bright things hanging on either side of her. They were beautiful gold and blue, and they bore her up off of the twig. "I am flying!" she cried. "I am flying!" And she flew in the bright, warm sunshine to the green field to show all her old friends.

The Dragonfly Grubs [3]

David and his mother were spending the summer afternoon by the pond in the woods back of their home. David watched the beautiful blue and green dragonflies darting and swirling in circles over the water.

"Mother, why do the dragonflies always stay near the water?" asked David. "Do they like to see their beautiful wings in the water?"

"Perhaps," said his mother, as she closed her book, "but I have just been reading about dragonflies, and I like to imagine it is another reason which draws them to the water. The pond, you see, was their home before they came to live in the world above."

"The muddy pond!" exclaimed David in surprise. "How could they live in the water with their beautiful wings?"

[3] From *Pilgrim Elementary Teacher,* The Pilgrim Press. Adapted from "Not Lost But Gone Before" in *Parables from Nature* by Mrs. Alfred Gatty.

"They didn't have wings then," replied his mother. "They were small brown grubs," and she showed him a picture in her book.

"Tell me more about them," eagerly begged David.

"I'll tell you a story I have imagined about a family of dragonfly grubs in our pond," said his mother. So David settled down to listen while he watched the dragonflies darting here and there over the surface of the water. And this is the story he heard.

In the bottom of a pond lived a family of nine brother grubs. They had a busy life in "the world," as they called their pond. All day they swam about hunting for food, for like most growing children they were generally hungry. They were so interested in their life in the bottom of the pond that they rarely looked up; but when they did, the surface of the water must have looked to them very much as the sky does to us. When darkness came over it they slept in the soft mud at the bottom of the pond; for like other children they, too, needed a great deal of sleep.

Had you asked them about their life, and they could have talked, I'm sure they would have told you that it was a very happy one. That is—they would have said this until one sad day when one of the brothers disappeared. This was the way it happened. In the morning when they had started out to hunt for breakfast he had complained that he felt sleepy and had climbed up one of the stalks of bulrushes. They supposed that he was going up nearer the warm sunbeams to take a nap; but higher and higher up the stalk he climbed, up to the very top of their world, and then he disappeared from sight. The eyes of the grubs could not see beyond the surface of the water, so they did not know where their brother had gone. They waited anxiously for him to come back. But when darkness came he had not returned. It was a sad family that went to bed that night, but in the morning one of the brothers had a bright idea. "Let's ask the frog," he said. "We have often seen him disappear from the world, then *splash* goes the water and he is back again. Perhaps he can tell us where our brother has gone."

They hurried in search of the frog; but when they found him sitting upon a rock it wasn't easy to question him. Had they not been so worried about their brother, I am sure, they would have swum away without disturbing him. Finally one of the brothers said, in his most polite voice, "Please, Mr. Frog, would you be so kind—" but when he saw the frog slowly turn his goggle eyes upon him, he stopped speaking.

"Why don't you finish your sentence?" asked the frog, for he was amused to have so tiny a creature try to talk to him. So the grub began again and said, "Would you be so kind, Mr. Frog, as to tell us where you go when you leave the world?"

"Leave the world?" asked the frog.

"Yes, when you disappear out of the world," said the grub, "where do you go?"

"What world do you mean?" asked the frog.

"Why, this world, of course, the world we live in," answered the grub, thinking the frog a little stupid.

"Oh, you mean this *pond*," laughed the frog. "So you think this pond is all the world! Why, my little fellow, there is a great world above it much more wonderful than anything in this pond. So you thought this pond was all the world!" and he swayed from side to side with laughter.

"Please tell us," begged one of the grubs, "has our brother who disappeared up a stalk gone to this great world of which you speak?"

Then the frog saw that the grubs were in distress, and, as he was really a kindhearted fellow, he stopped laughing and said: "You don't need to worry about your brother, my grub friends. I can tell you all about him. He's having a much better time than if he were still in this pond. Why, he's a dragonfly now! He has wings! He can fly! Why someday, little grubs, you, too, will be dragonflies, floating about through the air above." And he began to tell them about all the wonderful things they would see and do then. But they didn't know what he meant by "air" or "wings" and "flying." And the more the frog talked about the wonders of the world above, the more puzzled grew the grubs.

"I can't understand a word you're saying," one of the grubs finally told him. "It doesn't sound sensible. I believe you're making it up."

"He's teasing us," said another, "and I'm not going to be made fun of. I don't believe there is a world greater than our own."

But one of the brothers said: "I'm going to believe it. The frog is wiser than we are, and there are lots of things we can't understand. I like to think that our brother has gone to a place which is even more wonderful than this world we know, and that someday we'll go and see him again." And even when his brothers and friends laughed at him he said, "I'm going to believe."

And not long afterward, when the grubs were mourning for another brother who had climbed up a stalk and disappeared, he said, "Why should we be sad and want him to come back when he has gone to a world more wonderful than this?" But only a few of the grubs would believe and be comforted.

Then one day when he felt himself growing sleepy and at the same time had a desire to climb up a stalk nearer the warm sunbeams, he was not afraid. "Perhaps," he told himself, "I, too, am going into the world that is more wonderful than this," and he pushed higher and higher up the stalk until he hit the surface of the water. He felt very weak then, but he gathered up all his strength and pushed a little bit farther. Then he found himself in a stranger place than he could ever have imagined. There was no water pressing around him. There seemed to be nothing about him. Then he heard something crack and he found himself using all the strength he had left to struggle from something that seemed to be binding him. And the next thing he knew he saw himself, or rather what he had always thought was himself, clinging motionless to the stalk. He looked at his new self and thought that surely he must be dreaming. The warm sun had dried two strange things fastened to either side of him, and he saw that they were beautiful blue and green.

"Lift up your wings and fly," said a voice above him. He looked up and saw several beautiful creatures like himself. "Welcome, brother," they cried. "We have been waiting for you. Come, we will show you the wonders of this world." So he spread his wings. They bore him up off the stalk and he flew with his brother dragonflies in the bright sunshine to the meadow where there were flowers and birds.

But in the dragonflies' happy exploring of their new world they did not forget their brothers and friends in their old home below. Always they came back to the pond and flew near the surface of the water. That was why when each of the remaining brothers pushed his way up into the world above they were there to welcome him to the new life.

"Wasn't it funny, Mother," said David, "that the grubs thought their pond was all the world?"

"Yes," said his mother, "it was funny. Yet some people think that the world we can see with our eyes is all there is."

David looked at the beautiful blue and green dragonflies darting here and there over the sunlit water. "There are so many wonderful things in the world to see, Mother," he said, "and—I wonder about the world that we can't see."

STORIES ABOUT DEATH AND LIFE

New Clothes for Old [1]

Charles had a new suit of clothes. It was blue and fitted him exactly.

"What a pretty suit!" everybody said when he wore it the first time. "How well it fits, and how nice Charles looks in it!"

He wore it for a long time. Grandma Sterling who lived next door used to say, "I do love Charles in that blue suit!" But it was not the blue suit she loved, it was the boy inside it.

He wore the blue suit a long time, so long that it was like a part of Charles and people knew him by his blue suit.

By and by a button came off and another had to be sewed on. Then one day when he was playing he tore a big three-cornered tear in it.

"Your blue suit can't go out and play for a few days," his mother said. "It's sick, and has to go to bed and have the doctor!"

Charles laughed, for he knew what she meant was that it had to go to the tailor's and be mended.

After a few days it came back and it was almost as good as new.

Then the lining of his sleeve ripped, and Charles couldn't tell where to put his arm through. His mother

[1] Jeanette Perkins Brown. From *Pilgrim Elementary Teacher*, The Pilgrim Press.

had to mend it. Then two more buttons came off and the lining of his cuffs began to look frayed. His mother sewed on some new buttons and put new pieces in the cuffs. Then a hole came in the knee of his trousers and his mother had to patch them.

He did not play all the time now. He worked and helped his mother. He could run faster and do her errands, for his legs were longer. He could lift heavy things for her for his shoulders were broader and his arms were stronger. Once, in carrying an armful of wood, he stretched his suit so that it split up the back.

"Charles has outgrown his blue suit," said his father. "He needs another."

"Yes, it is quite worn out, too," said his mother. "I shall put it away. He won't need it any more."

When Grandma Sterling heard he was to have a new suit, she said, "I shall be sorry to see his blue suit go; I always liked him in it." But it was not the suit she liked, it was the boy inside it. For when the new suit was bought—a brown one this time—she said, "What a pretty suit that is! I thought I liked him in blue, but I love him in brown!"

One day Grandma Sterling was quite sick. A doctor came. She was often sick, and the doctor came and made her well for a while, then something would be the matter again. This time he could not make her well. Charles came running into the house.

"Mother," he cried, "Betty says Grandma Sterling is dead. She's not alive any more and they're going to carry her away!"

His mother said, "The Grandma Sterling you loved isn't dead, Charles. She's gone to live with God. What they are carrying away is the body she lived in. She isn't there."

Then his mother went and opened the drawer where his old blue suit lay.

"Remember how Grandma Sterling used to say," she asked, "that she loved you in that blue suit? But it wasn't the suit she liked. That is all worn out now. She loved the little boy inside it and he is the same, no matter what suit he has on.

"It was only Grandma Sterling's body that they carried away," she said. "It was old and worn out. It kept getting out of order and the doctor had to keep patching it up, and mending it, just as I had to keep patching up and mending your blue suit. By and by it couldn't be mended any more, just as your old suit couldn't be. Then your father bought you a new suit. But it is the same little boy inside it that was in the old. God has given Grandma Sterling a new kind of body, fresh and strong and one that won't get out of order. We don't know what it is like. That is one of the surprises God keeps for us until we go to him. But we know that Grandma Sterling is the same Grandma Sterling inside that we knew and loved."

Charles said, "Oh, I'm glad. I'll go and tell Betty." For he wanted Betty to know that what they loved about Grandma Sterling was somewhere living still.

Grampa Goes Home [2]

Randy and Margie were in the living room playing records on their record player when the telephone rang.

[2] Gordon T. Charlton, Jr. in *God Is with Us,* Department of Christian Education of the National Council of the Protestant Episcopal Church. Copyright © 1962 by The Seabury Press, Inc.

John and Jane and Betty were in their rooms studying. Randy's father answered the phone and then called Randy's mother.

When he came back into the living room, Randy's father said to Randy and Margie, "Better turn off the records for a few minutes. This is a long distance call and Mommy might have some trouble hearing."

Randy couldn't think of anything else to do for a minute, so he walked out into the hall where his mother stood, holding the telephone to her ear. He could see that she was listening closely. Randy thought she looked very worried.

Finally Randy's mother said in a quiet voice, "All right, Mother, we'll wait to hear from you again. Let us know when we should come. And tell Grampa we love him."

Randy thought his mother's voice sounded funny, and he saw that she had tears in her eyes. His father had come into the hall, and he also had a worried look on his face.

Randy began to feel afraid, though he didn't know why.

His mother hung up the phone.

"It's Grampa," she said.

Randy's father put his arms around Mother and led her into the living room. They walked right by Randy and didn't seem to notice him. Randy felt very small and lonely. He followed them into the living room, where they sat down together on the couch talking in very low voices. Margie started to put a record on and then didn't.

John and Jane and Betty seemed to hear that something was different, so they came in, too.

"What's the matter, Mommy?" Randy asked in a trembling voice. He could see from his mother's surprised look that she really had forgotten for a minute that he was there.

"Come here, Randy, and sit between us," his mother said, wiping her eyes on the back of her hand. "The rest of you sit close to me—on the floor is the only place, I guess."

Randy felt much safer when he was sitting between his mother and father.

"We think—we think . . ." Randy could tell it was hard for his mother and father to talk. But his mother went on. "Grampa is so sick he can't get well, we think," she said.

His mother stopped. Everyone was quiet.

Randy thought about it for a few minutes.

"You mean he is going to die and go to heaven?" he asked.

"Yes, we think so," said his mother.

"Won't we see him any more?" asked Randy.

"Not in this world where we live now," his mother answered.

Lots of questions went around in Randy's mind, questions such as, "Where is heaven? How far is it? What is it like? And why do you have to die to go there?" But he had asked his mother and father all these questions before, and he still wasn't exactly sure of the answers. After talking about heaven awhile, they always said, "I don't know, Randy, but God knows, and he will take care of us."

Randy wasn't afraid any more. But he still wondered what heaven was really like.

"Why are you crying?" he asked his mother.

"Because I will miss Grampa and because Grandmother will be lonesome for him until they are together again."

Randy's father said, "We can't help being sad, Son, even though we know that Grampa is going to his heavenly home."

Randy thought for a long time, and then he said, "We'd better tell God that Grampa is coming so he can get ready for him."

Randy's mother and father looked at each other for a second. Then his father said, "All right, Randy, you tell him for us."

"Well," began Randy, "I'm not sure what to say . . ." but he began, "O God, our heavenly Father, our Grampa is sick." Randy went on, "And he's going to die—and we love him. Will you please take care of him? For Jesus' sake. Amen."

Margie and Jane, and John and Betty, and Mother and Daddy all said the ending words, "For Jesus' sake. Amen."

A Story That Has No End
(*The Easter Story*)

Peter, James, and John and the other disciples were very sad. Jesus was dead. It was hard to believe. Though Jesus had told them when they were going up to Jerusalem that he would be put to death, they would not believe it. They did not think it could happen to Jesus. They could not understand why Jesus had let himself be taken and put to death. He could have prevented it; that they knew. He had deliberately gone up to Jerusalem where his enemies were, knowing that they were plotting his death. When the soldiers came for him, Peter drew his sword, but Jesus told him to put it up and let them take him. Jesus had great power; many times they had seen him use his power to help others, but he would not use it to save himself. Now he was dead. They had seen his body taken down from the cross Friday afternoon, put in a tomb, and the tomb sealed with a large stone. They were very sad and they were afraid.

All day Saturday, with fear in their hearts, they stayed indoors, talking, wondering, weeping with sorrow. They could not understand. They had expected Jesus to establish the kingdom of God he had proclaimed. In this kingdom they were to have been his special helpers. For this purpose they had left their homes and their work to follow him. It was for this that they had been preparing themselves the three years that they had been with Jesus. Now all was ended. Jesus was dead. They were left alone.

Before dawn the next day, the mother of James and John, with Mary Magdalene and some other women who loved Jesus, prepared spices and ointment to anoint his body. There had been no time for this loving service for him before his body had been placed in the grave, for the Sabbath had begun, when no work could be done. As soon as it was light they took the spices and went out to the tomb.

Suddenly Mary came running back from the tomb. The disciples looked at her in wonderment, for her face shone with great joy.

"Jesus is alive!" she cried. "I have seen him! He called me by my name! He said to tell you he would see you in Galilee."

The disciples listened with amazement, but they did not believe what Mary told them.

That night, when they were in the house with the door closed for fear of their enemies, Jesus came to them. He stood in their midst and said: "Peace be with you. As the Father has sent me, even so I send you."

Wonder and joy filled the hearts of the disciples. It was true! Jesus was alive! He had not left them! They were not alone! Then they remembered how he had told them that he must suffer and die, but that he would rise on the third day.

Many times during the weeks that followed, Jesus showed himself to his disciples; once to two of them as they walked by the way, again to all of them when they were in a home, another time when Peter, James, and John were fishing on a lake. And finally he came to them in Galilee as he had promised. The disciples were on a mountain where they had often been with Jesus. Jesus came and said to them: "Go . . . and make disciples of all nations, . . . teaching them to observe all that I have commanded you; and lo, I am with you always."

Then Jesus disappeared from their sight. Great joy was in the hearts of the disciples. Now they knew that Jesus would be with them in a new and wonderful way. They did not expect to see him again with their eyes; but they knew that now, because he had risen, he could be with them and with all his disciples always, wherever they were.

At last they understood that the kingdom Jesus came to establish was a kingdom of peace and love; it had to begin in the hearts of men. For this kingdom Jesus had lived; for it he had suffered and died and risen again. Now he was depending on them to carry on his work. They knew that they could, because always they could count on him to be with them, giving them the strength they needed.

And this is what happened. They returned to Jerusalem, the very city where Jesus had been put to death. No longer were they afraid; they stood up boldly and proclaimed the joyful news that Jesus had risen. When officers commanded them to speak no more in the name of Jesus, they said, "We cannot but speak of what we have seen and heard." And, although at times they were put in prison, they went right on preaching about the risen Jesus and teaching all that he had said and done. Many people in the city who had known Jesus, and many who had not, became his disciples.

Then Peter, James, and John and the other disciples went out into the world with the good news. Everywhere they went, people became Jesus' disciples.

This is a story that has no end. Down through the years Jesus' disciples have gone throughout the world to spread his kingdom; that is why we are his disciples. And today and tomorrow he is saying to us: "Go and make disciples of all nations, . . . and lo, I am with you always."

SUGGESTED ACTIVITIES: EXPERIENCING LIFE AND DEATH WITH CHILDREN

(See Chapter 4)

Watching Seeds Sprout. Cut a clean, white blotter the size and shape to fit inside a drinking glass, covering the sides of the glass. Place four dried lima beans or peas between the blotter and the glass, about halfway up and as far apart as possible. Then pour enough water into the glass to stand about an inch in the bottom of the glass after the blotter is soaked. Place the glass in a window; add water when needed to keep the blotter moist. In several days the dried bean or pea will change into a growing seedling plant; both the root and the stem can be recognized. Since the only supply of food for the plant is in the seed, after a few days it will begin to die unless it is planted in soil.

Observing a Caterpillar Become a Butterfly. To watch what was a crawling caterpillar emerge from its chrysalis a beautiful, four-winged butterfly is an exciting and inspiring experience. It is well worth the weeks of waiting. The food the caterpillar will need until it forms its chrysalis or cocoon (a butterfly forms a chrysalis, a moth spins a cocoon) will depend upon the kind of caterpillar you choose. The kind of food can be told by the plant upon which the caterpillar is found. The black swallowtail caterpillar (green and black stripes with yellow dots) can be found in gardens where carrots, celery, and parsley are grown; it feeds on the leaves of those plants. The famous monarch is one of the most beautiful butterflies, and interesting to learn about because of its long migrations. The caterpillar (striped like a zebra with gold spots) can be found wherever there are milkweed plants.

Put the caterpillar on the leaf on which it is found and a short stick in a large glass jar; punch plenty of holes in the lid of the jar to provide good ventilation. See that it has fresh food and occasionally add a few drops of water. If there is not some moisture, the butterfly's wings will be shriveled. Many good, illustrated books about this attractive insect can be obtained from your public library.

Looking at Nature Films. Almost all public libraries have access to 16mm films and filmstrips; more and more 8mm film loops will be available through public libraries for individual use. Watch for good nature movies on television, especially on the educational networks.

Making Charts or Posters to Show Cycles. Children enjoy illustrating the series of orderly changes in plants, butterflies and frogs, the seasons, a day, and growth changes in their own lives.

Experimenting with a Prism. Children can learn what makes the various colors in the sunset by using a prism. By holding a triangular glass prism in the path of a ray of sunlight, they can see for themselves that the light, which looks colorless, when it passes through the prism breaks up into six colors—violet, blue, green, yellow, orange, and red. They will have fun throwing the spectrum of color on various objects such as a white wall, a glass of water, snow, or flowers. They will discover that when they look at an object through a side of the prism, they see the spectrum colors. They can then understand how tiny particles of water in the evening sky act as little prisms separating the sunlight into various colors, and how the colors are reflected down to us by clouds just as the spectrum is reflected on the wall. They will understand, also, why rainbows appear in the sky after a rain when the sun begins to shine and little drops of water are still in the air.

Making Microscope Discoveries. Looking at a drop of stagnant water through a microscope, the children will be surprised to see tiny living creatures dividing in two. Other interesting things to observe are small flowers, feathers, parts of insects, molds, etc.

Playing with Magnets can be much fun, and the children will learn about the mysterious unseen power in a magnet. They can gather all kinds of trinkets and discover which ones a magnet will pick up; have them stroke a magnet a number of times with a darning needle, always rubbing it in the same direction, and discover that it can then pick up another needle. Yet the magnet has lost none of its power by giving some of it away. Help them find the northern and southern poles in the magnet; show them how to make a compass by floating a magnitized darning needle on a small sponge or cork in a pan of water and learn how dependable a magnet is in always pointing north. New magnets can be made by rubbing a piece of iron on a magnet or by keeping it in contact with the magnet for a long time. With two magnets the children can invent various games. They might make a puppet show. Puppet figures can be made out of nails with broad heads, using pipe cleaners for arms and heads and dressing them in cloth or paper. Trees and other scenery should be made out of materials which the magnets will not pull. For a stage, place a piece of glass (cover the edges with gummed tape to prevent a cut) between two tables. The "people" can be moved around on the stage by holding the magnets underneath the glass.

Making a Weather Indicator. A "weather flag" can be made from a piece of white blotting paper (about 4 x 2 inches). Wet the blotting paper with a solution of three parts water and one part cobalt chloride (this should be in a glass or porcelain container; it will eat into metal); then place it on a pad of newspaper to dry. When it is dry, glue one of the short ends to a popsicle stick or fasten it to the stick with masking tape. Because cobalt chloride is pink when wet and blue when dry, the flag will be blue in dry weather and pink when wet weather is coming.

Playing with the Wind. Wind chimes or stripes of colored tissue paper hung in a breezy place make children conscious of the movement of the air. They enjoy making windmills, flying kites, balloons, blowing soap bubbles and watching the wind carry them away.

Preparing Nesting Materials for Birds. Pieces of bright yarn, stripes of cloth, and string can be put through a plastic mesh scouring pad. Tie it to a bush or tree where the birds can see it and the children can observe them from a window.

Keeping a Wonder Table. Children like to have a special table upon which they can place the treasures they find or are given—sea shells, rocks, a bird's nest, new leaf buds, flowers, etc. If a magnifying glass is kept on this table, it will encourage close examination of their discoveries.

Learning About Wilson Bentley's Experience.

Wilson Bentley grew up in Vermont, where there is a great deal of snow in winter. When Wilson was a boy he had many good times playing in the snow. He liked to watch the snowflakes floating down around him. When they fell on his coat sleeve he thought they looked like beautiful little stars. He tried to draw pictures of them, but they would melt before he could finish his picture. When he was a little older and owned a camera, he tried to photograph snowflakes; always they melted before he could get their picture.

But Wilson kept trying, and when he grew up and learned more about taking pictures, he succeeded. He became the first person ever to photograph snowflakes. The pictures he took showed that each snowflake was in the form of either a three- or a six-pointed star. During the next forty years Wilson Bentley took over four thousand pictures of snowflakes. All were beautiful star-shaped designs, and he discovered that no two were ever alike.

Many of his pictures were printed in magazines. Scientists came to see him. Lace-makers began copying the star patterns in lace, and artists who worked in silver and gold used many snowflake designs in jewelry.

Your public library should have or be able to get for you his book, *Snow Crystals,* with photographs which should have fascination for children of any age.

Going on Expeditions to a farm, dairy, the zoo, a botanical garden or a greenhouse, a natural history museum, etc., are enjoyable experiences and provide opportunities for direct learning about the cycles of growth and change in living things.

Corresponding with Other Children. Children enjoy writing letters and exchanging pictures with other children whom they learn about but may not know. Contacts with children of other races, cultures, and backgrounds enlarge children's capacities for understanding and friendship. Groups in schools often enjoy exchanging letters. Mission boards can supply names and information about various schools, hospitals, and orphanages. Sometimes names of individual children who would like a "pen pal" can be obtained through teachers, missionaries, children's periodicals, or local newspapers.

Visiting a Settlement House, Mission, Lighthouse for the Blind, etc. Through such experiences children learn about people in different situations and their needs. They also have an opportunity of meeting dedicated persons who are working to make today's world a better place for others.

Participating in Service Projects gives children the experience of doing something concrete to help where there is need. In addition to the home and overseas mission boards of your own church, many organizations will send material giving definite suggestions of ways in which children can participate. Three organizations which can be contacted in care of the National Council of Churches, 475 Riverside Drive, New York 10027, are:

1. Church World Service; ask for pamphlets about S.O.S. (Share Our Surplus) and C.R.O.P. (Christian Rural and Overseas Program).
2. Ministry to Migrants, The Migrant Ministry Section, Room 552.
3. World Literacy and Christian Literature; ask for information about the "Lit-Lit" project.

Other organizations which can be helpful are:

American Bible Society
1865 Broadway
New York   10022

Heifer Project, Inc.
45 Ashby Road
Upper Darby, Pennsylvania   19082

UNESCO Gift Coupon Office
Room 2201 United Nations
New York   10017

PRAYERS

Let Us Pray [1]

Let us pray, for God loves us;
Let us pray, for God hears us;
Let us pray, for God is our God,
And we are all his children.

God Is My Strength [2]

In the day of trouble
I will call upon you, O God,
For you will answer me.
God is my help and strength,
A very present help in trouble.
Therefore I will not fear.
I will give thanks unto thee,
O God, for thou comfortest me.
I will trust and not be afraid,
For God is my strength.

[1] From *Tell Me About Prayer* by Mary Alice Jones. Copyright ©
1948 by Rand McNally & Company.

[2] Adapted from the Psalms.

To Know the Way [3]

In the morning, O Lord,
Let me feel Thy loving kindness,
For in Thee do I trust;
Cause me to know the way
Wherein I should walk;
Teach me to do Thy will;
For Thou art my God.

The World One Neighborhood [4]

We thank Thee, Lord, for eyes to see
    the beauty of the earth;
For ears to hear the words of love
    or happy sounds of mirth;
For minds that find new thoughts to think,
    new wonders to explore;
For health and freedom to enjoy
    the good Thou hast in store.

O may our eyes be open, Lord,
    To see our neighbors' need.
And may our ears be kept alert
    Their cries for help to heed;
Make keen our minds to plan the best
    for one another's good,
That all the world shall be at last
    One friendly neighborhood.

[3] Adapted from the Psalms.

[4] From *As Children Worship* by Jeanette E. Perkins. Copyright, 1936, 1964, The Pilgrim Press. Used by permission.

For Our Tongues [5]

O God, keep us free
From all untrue and unkind words;
Help us to use the gift of speech
To help others
And to give thanks to you
For all your goodness to us.
Keep us sometimes quiet and silent,
That our hearts and our minds
May listen to your voice.

Help Me to Grow [6]

Give me clean hands, clean words, and clean thoughts;
Help me to stand for the hard right against the easy
wrong;
Save me from the habits that harm;
Teach me to work as hard and play as fair in thy sight
alone as if all the world saw;
Forgive me when I am unkind, and help me to forgive
those who are unkind to me;
Keep me ready to help others at some cost to myself;
Send me chances to do some good every day;
Help me to grow more like Christ. Amen.

[5] Adapted from *Prayers New and Old* (Forward Movement Publications).

[6] Adapted from a prayer by William De Witt Hyde.

ENRICHING MATERIALS
FOR ADULTS

NEW TESTAMENT TEACHING ABOUT LIFE AFTER DEATH

I. *Life which is eternal is life lived in fellowship with God and other people.*

"What shall I do to inherit eternal life?" was the question asked of Jesus.

> You shall love the Lord your God with all your heart, and with all your soul, and with all your strength, and with all your mind; and your neighbor as yourself . . . Do this, and you will live.
> —Luke 10:25-27

These two commandments are laws of relationship; their essence is love. In the keeping of them we have life which is eternal. This eternal life begins here and now.

We know, however, that we have failed to love God with all our heart, soul, strength, and mind, and to love our neighbor as ourself.

> All have sinned and fall short of the glory of God.
> —Romans 3:23

> If we say we have no sin, we deceive ourselves, and the truth is not in us.—I John 1:8

In the New Testament it is not physical death which is significant, but moral and spiritual death.

> The sting of death is sin.—I Corinthians 15:56a

> The wages of sin is death.—Romans 6:23a

II. *There is grace—forgiveness.*

The sinner can be forgiven, restored to fellowship, and given a new start.

> Though sin is . . . wide and deep, thank God his grace is wider and deeper still! The whole outlook changes—sin used to be the master of men and in the end handed them over to death: now grace is the ruling factor, with righteousness as its purpose and its end the bringing of men to the eternal Life of God through Jesus Christ our Lord.—Romans 5:20-21 (Phillips)

> He has delivered us from the dominion of darkness and transferred us to the kingdom of his beloved Son, in whom we have redemption, the forgiveness of sins.—Colossians 1:13-14

III. *The nature of our experience at death will be the result of the nature of our thinking in this life and at the moment of death.*

In the Old Testament we are told, "As he thinketh in his heart, so is he."—Proverbs 2:7 (KJV)

Jesus said:

> There is nothing outside a man which by going into him can defile him; but the things which come out of a man are what defile him.—Mark 7:15

> Do you not know that you are God's temple and that God's Spirit dwells in you?—I Corinthians 3:16. (See also Matthew 6:24; Luke 6:43; John 15:1-6; I Corinthians 6:19.)

To the penitent thief on the cross Jesus said:

> Today you will be with me in Paradise.—Luke 23:43

IV. *We shall have a spiritual body.*

"How are the dead raised? With what kind of body do they come?" are the questions Paul deals with in the fifteenth chapter of I Corinthians. (This chapter also contains the first written account of Christ's resurrection, verses 3-8.) Paul says:

> What you sow does not come to life unless it dies. And what you sow is not the body which is to be, but a bare kernel. . . . So it is with the resurrection of the dead. What is sown is perishable, what is raised is imperishable. It is sown in dishonor, it is raised in glory. It is sown in weakness, it is raised in power. It is sown a physical body, it is raised a spiritual body. If there is a physical body, there is also a spiritual body.
> Lo! I tell you a mystery. . . . We shall all be changed. . . . For this perishable nature must put

on the imperishable, and this mortal nature must put on immortality. When the perishable puts on the imperishable, and the mortal puts on immortality, then shall come to pass the saying that is written:

"Death is swallowed up in victory."
—I Corinthians 15:36-37, 42-44, 51, 53-54

The men and angels who appeared at Jesus' birth, Transfiguration, Resurrection, Ascension, and to Cornelius and Peter, had bodily forms (Luke 1:5-19, 26-33; 9:28-33; 24:1-8; Mark 16:1-7; Acts 1:1-11; 10:1-8; 12:1-10).

V. *We shall recognize each other.*
Peter, James, and John recognized Moses and Elijah at the Transfiguration (Luke 9:28-33).

Jesus was recognized by his disciples after his resurrection (John 20:19-21).

Stephen at his martyrdom saw Jesus in heaven (Acts 7:55-56).

VI. *The "dead" are aware of those living in this world and are still affected by our prayers, thoughts, and attitudes.*

We are "surrounded by . . . a cloud of witnesses" (Hebrews 12:1a).

The parable of Lazarus and the rich man illustrates this (Luke 16:19-31).

"In heaven—there is rejoicing . . . over one sinner whose heart is changed" (Luke 15:10 Phillips).

VII. *The nature of life in the next world is revealed.*
We shall:

1. Continue to become, and we shall grow in fellowship with God.

   We are God's children now; it does not yet appear what we shall be, but we know that when he appears we shall be like him, for we shall see him as he is.—I John 3:2

2. Be active—work, serve, worship, and intercede.

   Life implies activity, creativity; the principle of growth is inherent in all life. Jesus said, "My Father is working still, and I am working" (John 5:17). His words to his disciples on the night before his death, "I go to prepare a place for you," implied activity and progress. (John 14:2b.)

   In the parables of the talents and pounds, the reward of the faithful servant was greater opportunity (Matthew 25:14-23; Luke 19:12-19).

   The book of Revelation says, "His servants shall worship him, they shall see his face" (22:3b-4a).

   The writer to the Hebrews said of Christ: "He is able for all time to save those who draw near to God through him, since he always lives to make intercession for them" (7:25).

3. Know joy without tears.

   Behold, the dwelling of God is with men. He will dwell with them, and they shall be his people, and God himself will be with them; he will wipe away every tear from their eyes, and death shall be no more, neither shall there be mourning nor crying nor pain any more, for the former things have passed away.—Revelation 21:3-4

FROM PROSE AND POETRY

> Thus says the Lord . . .
> "Seek me and live."—Amos 5:4

You will seek me and find me; when you seek me with all your heart.—Jeremiah 29:13

The souls of the virtuous are in the hands of God,
no torment shall ever touch them.
In the eyes of the unwise, they did appear to die,
their going looked like a disaster,
their leaving us, like annihiliation;
but they are in peace. . . .
Their hope was rich with immortality. . . .
They who trust in him will understand the truth,
those who are faithful will live with him in love.
—The Book of Wisdom 3:1-3, 4*b*, 9*a* (*Jerusalem Bible*)

He will swallow up death in victory; and the Lord God will wipe away tears from off all faces.—Isaiah 25:8 (KJV)

> Thou dost show me the path of life;
>   in thy presence there is fullness of joy,
>   in thy right hand are pleasures for evermore.
>   —Psalm 16:11

Jesus said:

"This is eternal life, that they know thee the only true God, and Jesus Christ whom thou hast sent." —John 17:3

"I am the resurrection and the life; he who believes in me, though he die, yet shall he live, and whoever lives and believes in me shall never die."—John 11:25-26a

"Let not your hearts be troubled; believe in God, believe also in me. In my Father's house are many rooms. . . . I go to prepare a place for you. I will come again and will take you to myself, that where I am you may be also. . . . If you loved me, you would have rejoiced, because I go to the Father."—John 14:1-3b, 28b

None of us lives to himself, and none of us dies to himself. If we live, we live to the Lord, and if we die, we die to the Lord; so then, whether we live or whether we die, we are the Lord's. For to this end Christ died and lived again, that he might be Lord both of the dead and of the living.—Romans 14:7-9

For we know that if the earthly tent we live in is destroyed, we have a building from God, a house not made with hands, eternal in the heavens.—II Corinthians 5:1

It has been the human mind at its best, which has insisted most strongly upon the truth of immortality. The great poets, Homer and Virgil, Dante and Shakespeare, Milton and Wordsworth, Tennyson and Browning—how they all sang of a life beyond the grave! The great philosophers, Socrates and Plato, Kant and Hegel and Emerson, who have graven their names deep upon the pages of serious inquiry, how they clung to the idea of the persistence of the spiritual element in man! The great founders of religions, Zoroaster, Mohomet, Jesus of Nazareth, how strong and serene was their faith in the world to come! The great statesmen, who by the impress of their personalities have moulded the lives of nations, Cicero and Cromwell, Lincoln and Gladstone, how strong they were in their confidence that death does not end it all!—Charles Reynolds Brown

There is nothing more striking in the Bible than the calm familiar way with which from end to end it assumes the present existence of a world of spiritual beings always close to and acting upon this world of flesh and blood. . . . There is no reserve, no vagueness that would leave a chance for the whole system to be explained away into dreams and metaphors. The spiritual world, with all its multitudinous existence, is just as real as the crowded cities and fragrant fields and loud battlegrounds of the visible.—Phillips Brooks

They that love beyond the world cannot be separated. Death cannot kill what never dies. Nor can Spirits ever be divided that love and live in the same Divine principle; the root and record of their friendship. Death is but crossing the world, as friends do the seas: they live in one another still. For they must needs be present, that love and live in that which is omnipresent. In this divine glass they see face to face; and their converse is free as well as pure.

This is the comfort of friends, that though they may

be said to die, yet their friendship and society are, in the best sense, ever present, because immortal.—William Penn

From Snow-Bound

Who hath not learned, in hours of faith,
    The truth to flesh and sense unknown,
That Life is ever lord of Death,
    And Love can never lose its own!

              John Greenleaf Whittier

Immortal Living [1]

There is immortal living now and here,
A way of life beyond the bounds of space,
A spirit life transcending death's frontier,
Where man and God meet hourly face to face.
No Euclid's mind can demonstrate the sums
Proving the problems sprung from death and
    birth—
Faith in immortal living only comes
To those who live immortality on earth.
First life and then belief—as flowers blow
Before the ordered science of research;
First life and faith before mankind may know
The pillard structure of a living church.
I know that spirits pass the body's tomb
Freely from life—into God's other room.

           Harold Trowbridge Pulsifer

[1] By permission of the estate of Harold T. Pulsifer.

From Threnody

When frail nature can no more,
Then the Spirit strikes the hour:
My servant Death, with solving rite,
Pours finite into infinite.

What is excellent,
As God lives, is permanent;
Hearts are dust, hearts' loves remain;
Heart's love will meet thee again.

Ralph Waldo Emerson

Turn Again to Life

If I should die and leave you here a while,
Be not like others, sore undone, who keep
Long vigil by the silent dust and weep.
For my sake turn again to life and smile,
Nerving thy heart and trembling hand to do
That which will comfort other souls than thine;
Complete these dear unfinished tasks of mine,
And I, perchance, may therein comfort you.

Mary Lee Hall

A Letter

Perhaps this will help you now:

First: Whatever happens, life must go on for you. There are too many friends and loved ones depending on you to do otherwise. Whatever happens to us, the stream of life must flow on. So take good care of yourself and don't give way to total defeat. Much in life is for you and with you whatever comes. Keep this firmly fixed, these days.

Second: Don't give way to "what might have been." We are apt to do so. We are apt to think that if we had known sooner or if we had done differently, it would not be this way. But this is a region without boundary lines. It might not have changed results one bit. Don't linger there. You have done and are doing all you can in every way you know. Leave it there, for this is all any one of us can do in life.

Third: God is sad over this as you are. It is not God's will that such things happen. Amid the many circumstances of life, some things happen because we belong to a human society. But God's will is for life to be lived to its fullness. When it isn't, He stands as of old, weeping with us.

Fourth: We Christians believe in immortality. Whatever is commenced here will be completed there. *Nothing is lost* out of His care.[2]

---

[2] From a letter to Iona Henry written by her father-in-law when Mrs. Henry was facing the possible death from cancer of her fourteen-year-old daughter.

PRAYERS

Almighty God, we entrust all who are dear to us to thy never-falling care and love, for this life and the life to come; knowing that thou art doing for them better things than we can desire or pray for; through Jesus Christ our Lord. Amen.[1]

Lord of life and death and more abundant life, who hast set a door of birth leading from one into another; help us to keep our focus clear and sharp during this earthly span, distinguishing the real from the unreal, shadow from substance, so that entering into life Eternal our souls may be fully awake to the wonders that lie ahead.[2]

O Father of all, we pray thee for those whom we love, but see no longer. Grant them thy peace; let light perpetual shine upon them; and in thy loving wisdom and

---

[1] *Book of Common Prayer.*

[2] *Prayers and Meditations,* ed. by Gerald Heard, p. 138, Harper and Brothers, 1949.

almighty power work in them the good purpose of thy perfect will; through Jesus Christ our Lord. Amen.[3]

We seem to give them back to thee, dear God, who gavest them to us. Yet, as thou didst not lose them in giving, so we have not lost them by their return. Not as the world giveth, givest thou, O Lover of Souls! What thou givest, thou takest not away. For what is thine is ours always, if we are thine. And life is eternal: and love is immortal; and death is only a horizon; and a horizon is nothing save the limit of our sight. Lift us up, strong Son of God, that we may see further; cleanse our eyes that we may see more clearly; draw us closer to thyself, that so we may know ourselves nearer to our beloved who are with thee. And while thou dost prepare a place for us, prepare us for that happy place, that where they are and thou art, we too may be. Amen.[4]

O God, whose best gifts come always through the lives in which we see thee reflected, we bring thee our gratitude for all who have bequeathed to us a goodly heritage. We bless thee that those who have passed beyond our present sight are still of our unseen fellowship. We thank thee for their power still to touch our common days with sacredness, and our common tasks with meaning; to speak to our inmost souls their word of courage and hope,

[3] *Book of Common Prayer.*
[4] Rossiter W. Raymond.

and to quicken our faith in things unseen and eternal. Keep them in thine everlasting care, and help us to follow them more worthily through the life that now is and into that which is to come. Amen.[5]

Grant unto us, our Father, to live as those to whom has been given the power of an endless life. Help us to live the eternal life here and now—the life of faith, of love, of fellowship, of service. Make us to measure by eternal values and to live for eternal ends. So shall all of life be full of meaning, and of beauty.[6]

Life is a prayer; death, the benediction.[7]

[5] Charles W. Gilkey. Used by permission of his son, Langdon B. Gilkey.

[6] Margaret E. Burton, *Assurances of Life Eternal* (New York: Thomas Y. Crowell, 1959) , p. 94.

[7] Juliet H. Reed. From her notebook.